The Great Romance

The Sun Returns, Time Never

Also by Carl Vigeland

Great Good Fortune

In Concert

Stalking the Shark

Jazz in the Bittersweet Blues of Life (with Wynton Marsalis)

Letters to a Young Golfer

The Mostly Mozart Guide to Mozart

The Breathless Present

Jonathan Sternberg

The Great Romance

The Sun Returns, Time Never

Carl Vigeland

Photos on pages vii, 5, 8, 10, 21 26, 34, 67, 97,
and back cover by Carl Vigeland.

Levellers Press, Amherst, Massachusetts

Printed in the United States of America

ISBN 978-1-937146-61-0

Life is not a dress rehearsal.

—Mildred Elman

Sol redit, tempus nunquam. The sun returns, time never.

Contents

Prologue

Photo by Elizabeth Brooke

OVER THE YEARS, I'D HEARD BITS AND PIECES of stories about him. Once, years ago, at a concert of early music performed on period instruments, a friend pointed out the handsome, well-dressed man listening intently. "That's the owner, or producer...not sure what to call him. The patron." Someone else told me that he'd heard the guy was some kind of businessman in New York but he climbed mountains—high, famous mountains—and that was just one of his pastimes...passions, really. "You must have run into him somewhere, sometime, maybe here at Tanglewood," yet another acquaintance insisted. And the man's house...a showplace, nothing else like it. "I know," I thought, or rather, "I knew..."

But I didn't.

PART I
Looking Up

High Andes, 1993.

I. *A Dark Wood*

"Where can it be found again.
An elsewhere world, beyond
Maps and atlases,
Where all is woven into
And of itself, like a nest
Of crosshatched grass blades?"

—Seamus Heaney

Until I finally met Lee Elman, I thought that whoever wrote time heals all wounds must have had a very gentle muse. What would I know, I can imagine my late father saying.

It was Labor Day weekend, and I was early for an event at Tanglewood, the Boston Symphony Orchestra's summer home in the Berkshires of western Massachusetts. Tanglewood for me was consecrated ground because both my father and brother had studied there, and I'd spent much of my life listening to music within its so-called Shed or outside on the verdant expanse of its tree-shaded lawns.

Searching for something I could neither precisely define nor describe—call it the ghost of a feeling—I shunned the main road and drove from West Stockbridge through the nearby hamlet of Alford, looking first for an old inn that in my father's telling was the scene during his heyday of great parties, and then tracing the route of the Green River to a skinny dipping spot one of my father's old friends had told me about. My meanderings led me eventually to a hilltop park on the outskirts of trendy Great Barrington, once an outback and now a thriving center of chic restaurants and weekend retreats. I left my car and walked downhill by a lovely, fragrant meadow and then through some sun-dappled woods along a dirt road that ended at the river.

No naked people in the water that day, but the sound of the river running over rocks reminded me of a summer long past. I imagined I could hear my father's voice echoing over the gurgles and ripples of a white-foamed shallow pool in which he was standing, the water waist high, as he carried on an animated conversation with one of my college friends—this must have been 40 years ago, I calculated, when one of my father's old girlfriends had given our family her Great Barrington house for an entire summer while she and her dentist husband undertook an extended period of traveling. "Who knows a family as lucky as ours?" my father would say at such moments, and it was impossible as he spoke to know if this thought were a belief or a wish.

He could be like that. An organist and choir director, he was also a teacher, and he had a deep well of stories and anecdotes culled from a lifetime of wide reading to share with both his students and his children. Often, when he wished to explain something or simply make a point, instead of speaking directly, he would tell me a story from which I was supposed to divine a meaning or a message. A compulsive letter writer, who carried on correspondences with an enormous number and diversity of people, he wrote me long reports, complete with stories, beginning when I left home for college. It was people, he was forever reminding me, that other people want to hear about, an admonition he remembered when he was writing the text for a talk or an article in one of the professional journals he subscribed to. In my memory I could see his blue eyes staring intently at me, waiting for a response, some word or gesture on my part that signified recognition of the importance of what had just been imparted to me.

Already, as I made my way back up to my car, I knew where I wanted to go next. With directions starting on Main Street, a block past the Castle Street corner that led to the historic Mahaiwe Theater, near the town's train station, long out of service, I took the next right and continued uphill by Fairview Hospital. There, after a car accident the week before Thanksgiving in 1976 in Sheffield, a neighboring town to the south, my father was rushed by ambulance. His room looked out on the adjacent, lower, eastern perimeter of the Aston Magna grounds, a place that in our family lore had by then taken on the exalted status of myth.

Through a neighborhood of tidy middle class homes, I continued before turning at the last left onto Berkshire Heights, which brought me soon to an enormous strand of very tall, second-growth pine trees. The street ended there, but I kept going, just as I knew my father would have, past a sign that said, in small letters, "Private," and then in larger script, "Aston Magna." Along a winding, dirt and gravel driveway, framed by thousands of more trees, I drove by another sign on my left that said, "Stable," and soon thereafter, on my right, a large, log-framed lodge. Finally, I came to a sudden airiness and bright-ness that presaged a break in the forest. The road now made a hairpin turn as I reached an open place that in one direction revealed an expansive view of the southern Berkshires in what seemed their inviting, soothing entirety and in the other, across a long lawn, a legendary house.

I knew I should turn around. But something beyond mere curiosity compelled me to keep going. With a start, I began to question again what I might have missed when I was younger about who my father once was.

Around the turn a low stone wall marked the edge of the driveway on the driver's side and another part of the lawn that sloped downward toward what appeared to be an orchard of different kinds of fruit trees. A second sign a little farther ahead, where the driveway split in two directions, said, "One way," with an arrow pointing left.

My pulse quickening a little, I continued through an area with trees lining either side, the house on a slight rise to the right and a much steeper slope to the left, with what appeared to be a vineyard on the side of a western facing portion of the property. The driveway then slung around toward the right, well behind the rear of the house, with an enormous concrete holding tank—presumably for water—through more trees and more lawn to the left. To one side of the tank was a much smaller building that I neither recognized nor remembered. But as the driveway continued to the next side of the house, I was soon facing in the opposite direction from where I'd looked after the hairpin. I noticed another small building on my left— a guest house?—and wondered if down below it might be the swimming pool in which I first had been taken for a swim when I was only a couple of years old. Of course I had no memory of this; rather, what I recalled were the times my father would tell and retell the story, as if in some strange way it conferred upon him a blessing that, after his death, I had on occasion and, I now sensed, mistakenly interpreted as a curse.

Ahead, as I drove along the other side of the house, I saw the figures of two older women, sitting in wooden chairs facing out toward the main part of the lawn. Each of them reading, they both looked up as I stopped my car near them and got out.

"Excuse me," I said, "I'm so sorry. I didn't mean to disturb you." That was not exactly true, but I felt obliged to say something, though neither of the women seemed bothered by my sudden appearance. Perhaps this sort of thing happened often here.

Looking directly at me, one of the women smiled. I smiled back.

"What a beautiful place you live in," I said, and then gave my name. But before I could say anything more, the other woman told me this wasn't their house. "We're just guests," she said.

Relieved, I stepped forward and began to explain something about my father years ago, before the Second World War, when a famous violinist lived here—Albert Spalding was his name, I added, but with a nod from the second woman I realized this information was something they already knew.

"It's Lee Elman's house now," one of the women said.

"Is Mr. Elman around?" I asked.

"He must be someplace near. Know he's back from riding. Did you see the horses as you came in? Maybe he's swimming."

If I wrote a short note to Mr. Elman, I asked, would the women be kind enough to give it to him?

"Of course."

I returned to my car to get a pen and one of my business cards. Just as I had finished writing my message and began walking back toward the women, I heard steps behind me. I turned. There, standing before me, was a well tanned man with thinning hair, looking at me inquisitively but somehow still cordially. The man's feet were bare and, wearing only his bathing suit, he was dripping wet.

"Hello," he said, extending his right hand. "I'm Lee."

Shaking that hand, I returned Lee's smile and introduced myself, and with an apology for my intrusion repeated the story about my father that only a few minutes ago I had shared with the two women. This time I added some information about the basis of my father's relationship with Spalding, so far as I knew it.

"Your father was Spalding's accompanist?" Elman asked, somewhat incredulously. "I'll have to look up his name in Spalding's book."

"No, not accompanist," I replied. "Rehearsal pianist. And just for a short time...I'm not sure how long exactly, but it was before the war. World War Two."

And then I explained how my father had come up to the Berkshires from New York when he was only eighteen, found a job playing the organ in a local church, gave piano lessons, conducted a chorus in Pittsfield, and attended Tanglewood classes during the first summer of its student institute. Sometime before that he had been introduced to Spalding—I was not sure how—and that led to his engagement as occasional rehearsal pianist, when the great violinist wished to practice.

"Amazing!" Elman exclaimed, in a voice that was itself musical—a baritone, I thought—and with an inflection of interest so striking that someone else hearing it might have thought a special thing had just happened.

"So," Elman said, "can you stay for a swim?"

Had I brought along my suit and not been headed elsewhere, I might have accepted Elman's invitation. But my father had always preached tempo in whatever one did and with whomever one was. And I had a sixth sense that this was not the last time I would have such an opportunity. Elman asked for my phone number and I gave him the card on which I had been writing just a few minutes earlier.

"Are you sure you can't stay," Elman repeated. "You could join us for lunch," he continued, and nodded toward a roof-covered porch on one side of the house, where I could see a man with a chef's white hat tending to a grill.

"That's very kind," I said. "I can't today, but I live little more than an hour away, in Amherst, the college town. I come through here often—it's kind of a back way home for me if I've been in the city. I'll take the Taconic—no trucks—and then cut through Hillsdale and stop usually in South Egremont. Do you know the Old Mill, the place with the bar that seats four people and Adrian the bartender from South Africa who remembers everyone's names and drinks?"

"Of course!"

Another exclamation, which came across as genuine, as if I'd just shared some secret and my new acquaintance wanted to convey his gratitude.

"You've lived here long?" I asked.

"Since 1971," Elman said. "But I still drive up every weekend from New York."

I wanted to ask him what he did in New York, but that didn't seem appropriate at that moment. Instead, I started to tell Elman about the last time I'd been here, which I calculated was just a year before Elman took ownership. It was the summer we'd stayed at the house of my father's former girlfriend, located at the very bottom of the same hill on which Aston Magna was perched. Having survived her husband by 17 years, Spalding's widow had recently died. My father was pretty certain that the caretaker of Aston Magna would remember him if we were to drive up, and he did, in fact we stayed long enough for a swim.

Elman must have been a young man when he bought the place, I thought. And it must have been soon afterwards that the Aston Magna concerts began, an annual festival of early music performed on original instruments. When was that, I wondered aloud, addressing Elman as Lee.

"1972."

"But the concerts were not here?" I asked. "Because I'm sure I remember going to at least one at a church in town. In fact I may have written about it for a magazine."

"That would be Saint James, at the bottom of the hill," he answered. "But that was later. When we started the festival, the concerts were in the studio you might have noticed as you drove in. And the office was in the lodge," Lee added, nodding in the direction of the woods toward the left side of the lawn. "We called it the Patricia Lodge, in memory of my sister Patricia, who had just died."

"I'm so sorry," I said. "I didn't know."

"It's okay," said Lee. "It was a long time ago." As he spoke, some kind of a Labrador—yellow or white, it was hard to tell, since from its gait the dog seemed old—appeared and waited by Lee for a pat.

"This is Hanley," Lee aid. "One of my daughter's dogs."

"She lives here, too?" I asked. "What's her name?"

"Alex. She has an apartment on the second floor of the house. She comes up from the city now and then, with me or with her boyfriend."

"And she raises dogs?"

"No. Hanley was one of her service dogs. Now she has another, named General. Alex is blind."

Momentarily uncertain what to say, I finally uttered a quiet, "oh, my," and asked Lee if there were other children.

"No. She's my only one. An absolutely incredible woman.

When you come again you will have to meet her."

"I'll look forward to that," I said. "Can you tell me before I go, is Mr. Spalding's studio still being used?"

"No longer as a studio. Someone lives there now, a couple actually. Their main home is in Philadelphia. I converted the studio several years ago into a rental."

"I see," I said, as I tried to recall my father's descriptions of the room in which he had played with Spalding. How often had that happened? And what did it matter, the number? My train of thought was interrupted by Elman's excusing himself, saying he'd be right back, which indeed he was a few minutes later, carrying a bottle in one hand and a small paperback book in the other, with something else folded into it.

"This is just a picnic wine," Lee said, as he gave me the bottle, which was labeled Aston Magna, Cuvée Privée. "The grapes are from our vineyard but someone else makes the wine. And here's a cookbook of some of my favorite recipes, things I've served to guests over the years. You must promise to come back for dinner! Oh, and then there's a little something I wrote about Hemingway, whom I met in college and then a couple of times after."

Hemingway.

Alex.

Wine.

Music.

Food.

The house.

The grounds.

The view.

Who was this man who greeted a stranger with an invitation for lunch, who mourned a sister with a lodge named after her, whose great pride was an only child who had lost her sight, whose idea of a good time in his late 70s was to go on a morning-long horseback ride followed by a swim?

"Thank you," I said, shaking Lee's hand and then adding, "imagine...I almost turned around when I realized this was a someone's home. It's a little like that Frost poem, the one where two roads diverge in the woods."

"Yes," said Lee, "I know it well. But I'm thinking of a different poet." Whereupon, from memory, he recited the following:

> Nel mezzo del cammin di nostra vita
> mi ritrovai per una selva oscura,
> ché la diritta via era smarrita.

"It's Dante," he continued, smiling, when I failed to identify it. "The beginning of *The Divine Comedy*." Whereupon he added an English translation he'd also memorized:

> Midway this way of life we're bound upon
> I woke to find myself in a dark wood,
> Where the right road was wholly lost and gone.

Opening my car door, I looked up and out, across the lawn, past the trees that formed an irregular line across the low horizon, and then above and past the very wide valley. As someone might entering Notre Dame for the first time or climbing over the last dunes before viewing the ocean, I felt I was one step from heaven on earth.

Far off in the distance I could see the rounded peak of Mount Everett, with its outcroppings of rock on which I had first walked as a very young child, holding the hand of my happy father as we picked blueberries.

When at the age of 64 my father died of a heart attack in 1982, we scattered his ashes near that summit. From the shaded boulder we'd chosen as his final resting place, we could see several miles to the north one of the enormous lawns of Tanglewood, where his participation in 1940 as a member of the first conducting class that also included Leonard Bernstein and Lukas Foss had been made possible, I now remembered, with a recommendation from Albert Spalding.

Closer by, as I stood still, back then in the late August afternoon of an immense sadness, I was also able to make out the location of Aston Magna. I remember wondering if anyone were living there, but the wound from my father's demise was so deep that 30 years would pass before, finally at this moment, I found out the answer to my question.

If, as my father once told me, a person's life can change at any moment, I was learning again that it does not have to mean for the worse. Even a few words or a simple gesture may echo and resonate across human boundaries, my father said, and kindness divided without judgment or expectation will multiply itself beyond measure.

I closed my car door and, waving a goodbye, drove off. In my rear view mirror, I could see Lee, already in conversation with the two women in the chairs. I drove slowly until I reached the woods, where I pulled over and, leaving the car running in case someone were to approach, I leaned forward for a few seconds, with my forehead resting on the steering wheel.

I needed to breathe.

I wanted to shout.

I wanted to get out of the car and run…where?

I wanted to go back to that swimming hole, strip off my clothes, and jump in.

2. The Blue Room

"Because I am mad about women
I am mad about the hills."

—Yeats

PRESSED TO EXPLAIN HIMSELF, Lee says, "I'm no one special. There are lots of people like me."

None, I reply, whom I have ever met. None who on the marble coping by their swimming pool own a sacrificial altar from Herculaneum on which is engraved, "Sol Redit, Tempus Nunquam" ("the sun returns, time never"), which Lee claims as his philosophy, transliterating its meaning as "grab life by the balls."

Several months have passed since our first meeting, though we've stayed in touch via email, and he's invited me for dinner a couple of times. Once I had a conflict, and once I had to cancel because I wasn't feeling well.

It's an early spring morning. Waiting for two other luncheon guests, we are sitting on the front patio at Aston Magna, about which I've been exploring, seeking to explicate fact from fiction.

The story begins with a 19th-century industrialist and railroad baron, Charles Freer, whose art collection is today housed in the Freer Gallery of Art part of the Smithsonian Institution in Washington, D.C. Near the end of his life, Freer purchased property in Great Barrington and hired a noted architect, Charles Platt, to design a house that might also become a gallery. Construction was completed in 1918, but Freer did not live long enough to enjoy it; he died in 1919.

The beautiful place he had created would eventually attract the attention of Albert Spalding, who with his wife first in 1925 rented and then in 1929 bought the estate they renamed Aston Magna.

In New York City, Lee lives in what he describes as a small bachelor apartment on Park Avenue and runs a very successful real estate investment firm that specializes in buying properties that are leased to the federal government. A *magna cum laude* graduate of Princeton University's Woodrow Wilson School, with two law degrees from Yale University, Lee grew up in Mount Kisco, New York, where he was born on June 6, 1936. His father, a civil engineer, owned a Mount Kisco auto parts place, which is still in business today, though it is no longer in the family.

In addition to Patricia, Lee had two other sisters, all of whom have died. Lee attended the local high school and ran a thriving lawn-mowing businesses that paid for trips to Europe and college. He speaks five languages, has traveled all over the world, climbed to the North Col of Mount Everest in 1986, when he was 50 years old, plays tennis and fishes, and was once an expert skier. A past member of the New York State Council on the Arts—under Governors Mario Cuomo and Hugh Carey—as well as a former Commissioner of Cultural Affairs for New York City under Mayors Abe Beame and Ed Koch, he is acquainted with Madeleine Albright and Condoleezza Rice, former New York City Mayor Michael Bloomberg and Senator Charles Schumer, folksinger Arlo Guthrie, former baseball player and author Jim Bouton, Donald Trump, George Soros, playwright A.R. Gurney, and hundreds of other famous folk.

When Lee was a student at Princeton, an English professor referred him to a speech therapist named Madame Oppenheim for a stutter he had developed when he was ten, after his father suffered a nervous breakdown triggered by some financial difficulties. A member of the prominent Belgian family Errera, Madame Oppenheim had fled the Nazis in the late 1930s with her German husband Paul, escaping with an art collection that included a Monet that Paul had given her on the occasion of the birth of their first son. That son later died in the Coconut Grove fire in 1942; a second son became a professor at the University of Massachusetts at Amherst. Paul studied and wrote philosophy at Princeton's Institute for Advanced study, where one of his closest friends was Albert Einstein (who coincidentally used to come to Aston Magna to play violin with Spalding).

"More champagne?" Lee asks me, filling my glass before I have replied. We are actually drinking a cocktail called a Kir Royale, in which champagne has been mixed with a French liqueur, crème de cassis. Though it's quite chilly, Lee wears no jacket over his blue argyle sweater for extra warmth. He's still in his riding pants and boots from a two-hour ride with his regular riding buddies this morning.

Lee's companion, Judy Ney, whom I am meeting for the first time, comes out onto the terrace carrying a plate of cold, peeled shrimp and a dip that I take to be remoulade. It was Judy, a lovely woman with whom Lee has been together for three years (though in New York they keep separate apartments), who via her iPhone confirmed the arrangements for today's lunch. I have been waiting to ask her if she is related to the advertising executive Ed Ney, a man of regal bearing I once knew as a trustee of his alma mater, Amherst College.

"My former husband," Judy tells me. "He's not well," she adds with a sigh.

"What a beautiful couple they were," says Lee, with admiration. He seems genuinely happy to affirm the glamorous splendor of Judy's married state, as if he were celebrating a pleasant memory from his own life, which he confides in passing has included four marriages, "two official, two virtual."

I'm not sure at first whether to take this remark as a revealing confession or a humorous aside, and then it occurs to me that one doesn't necessarily cancel the other.

Just then, a car appearing at the rise in the driveway at the hairpin-turn end of the lawn indicates that the other guests are arriving. I'm a little bit anxious, wondering how the occasion will unfold. Lee barely registers a change in what I will come to recognize as a constant expression of interest with whomever he is speaking. Rising to greet a middle-aged couple—a local sculptor and his wife, a masseuse—whom he recently met at a party, he booms out a hearty, "welcome!"

Another bottle of champagne is opened by a woman who is helping in the kitchen, as Lee makes the introductions, perfectly remembering names and adding something complimentary about each person. To hear his description of me, it might seem I had just won a Pulitzer.

"My new literary agent," I say, smiling, but the line falls flat. No matter. We are taking seats as Judy announces it is too cold to remain outside for lunch. "Not that the temperature would matter to Lee," she adds. "We've sat out here many times in the middle of winter."

It's something I can't picture Albert Spalding and my father ever doing. But imagining my father doing anything just now, I am surprised to realize, is far from my mind. Where is the ghost, I wonder, who guided me here last fall?

"Lunch is served," Judy announces.

"Shall we check on the horses?"

This is a rhetorical question. We've finished our chicken salad and carrot cake, we've enjoyed our wine, and Lee has excused himself momentarily before returning with a box containing Cuban cigars, which he passes around to his guests as we drink our coffee. Tempted, I decline, as we linger at the large, rectangular table that fills the dining room. Overlooking us at the table is a mounted elk head that a friend gave him years ago.

Lee has offered to take us on a tour of the property, beginning with the pasture where his horses graze. Before we leave the table, Lee picks up the camera that he placed earlier by his plate and takes several photos of me and his other guests. A week or so later, a hand-addressed envelope from his New York office will arrive at our respective homes, with a printed card saying, "With compliments of Lee Elman," and several color prints from the occasion. I will soon learn this is a regular commemoration of every visit, just as, now, I discover upon exiting the dining room through an alcove leading to the living room that my new friend has a photographic archive on display of his life's passions—people he has known, places he has been, adventures he has enjoyed. There are framed photographs on the walls, on bookshelves, on tables, even on the piano that is tucked into a recessed corner by the main entrance to the house.

I want to stop and look more carefully, but that will have to wait. Time for our field trip, with the men in one car—Lee's dark blue Mercedes—and the ladies following in Judy's.

Past the stable, which Lee tells us he rescued from demolition and had brought to Aston Magna and rebuilt, piece by piece, we leave the property and head downhill, past the hospital but then taking a different turn than the one, coming from the other direction, that leads from downtown Great Barrington. Instead, we soon pass what I immediately recognize as the house once owned by my father's former girlfriend, the place where our family had stayed that entire summer, the year before Lee bought Aston Magna. Taking a right at the corner to the state highway, we continue at a fast clip little more than half a mile before another right brings us onto a dirt driveway.

Bouncing our way uphill, we shortly come to a large, fenced-in clearing on our left: the estate's lower pasture. There, grazing peacefully, are Lee's horses—three Thoroughbreds named Banner, Charlie, and Paprika, and a Morgan called Sebastian.

"This is where they'll spend the summer," Lee explains. "Isn't it romantic?"

Romantic. What has prompted this word, I wonder to myself. It's so unlike the vocabulary I would have associated with an image of thundering hooves and glistening sweat on a hot day and the smell of leather, the feel of stirrups and reins.

Silently, I watch Lee watch his horses. Then he takes us over to a small, nearby shed.

"My tack room," he says, and then adds proudly, "no lock."

Inside, hanging on the unpainted walls, is several thousand dollars worth of gear.

"You don't worry it's going to be stolen?" I ask.

"Never had a problem," Lee replies.

"Wow," I exclaim, but upon brief reflection I'm not really that surprised. In a way that is still coming to me, little by little, it seems in character. And it also seems, not naive but... romantic, which as I continue to think about it is how all those photographs in the living room struck me, not in other words as showing off but as a kind of joyful sharing of good fortune crossed with the spoils of ambition, hard work, and an extraordinary knack for getting along with other people...a gift, really.

And if this, too, were part of the romance, as of course it must be, could not the source at least in part be Lee's innate sense of something his fellow Princetonian, F. Scott Fitzgerald, once wrote, long before Lee studied there amidst the spires and gargoyles that Fitzgerald celebrated in his first book-length fiction?

"The sentimental person," according to the author of *This Side of Paradise* as well as the iconic *Great Gatsby*, "thinks things will last—the romantic person has a desperate confidence that they won't."

Desperate always struck me as the critical word, because it implied a degree of volition, an affirmation as it were of an insight that could not be proven but had to be lived.

Like horses, like photographs.

Like photographs, like hospitality.

Like hospitality, like...

...my thoughts are interrupted by a sharp but genial, "let's go!" Another trait revealed, not necessarily romantic: *don't stand in place* or, in the Italian he shared with me upon our first meeting, which I'm thinking could be another of his mottos: *avanti!*

In the Mercedes again, Lee chooses a different route for our return, over terrain more suited for a Jeep or tractor. Nor does he take things cautiously. If there were a posted speed limit on this private dirt road he would be breaking it—as, he laughs, he habitually does on the Taconic State Parkway, his preferred route to and from New York. I mention this later to Judy, who shakes her head affectionately as she tells me that Lee has received so many speeding tickets that he has a lawyer on retainer, just to deal with them.

"Once," she continues, "a condition of the judgment was that Lee would be required to attend what was called a traffic school. Which he did. Also present was the officer who had stopped him. Afterwards, Lee invited him here for dinner!"

Upon our return to the house, Lee and the sculptor leave me on my own while they walk to the front lawn, apparently to discuss the sculptor's suggestion that this would be an ideal location for one of his works.

"The back door is unlocked," Lee says. "I thought you'd like to see the portrait of Spalding that is hanging there."

Letting myself into the library where Lee has suggested, I'm immediately struck by a single name and a single word on a plaque next to the door: Patricia Lodge. This, I realize, must once have hung on the nearby lodge, originally called Logarythms when it was added to the estate in 1964 by Spalding's widow. Lee's late brother-in-law, Albert Bildner, made a gift that enabled the building to become the original headquarters for the concert festival and its attendant activities, which at various times included master classes and an academy. Those headquarters are now in downtown Great Barrington and the lodge was sold, with the proceeds used to establish an endowment for the Aston Magna Foundation.

Lingering briefly in this quiet space, where the portrait of Spalding casts a silent spell—no music—I breathe deeply as I exit and decide to continue my explorations outside. Walking toward the driveway, which I cross, I make my way slightly downhill, through some budding trees, and soon reach the pool, which this early in the season is still empty, save for some leaves from last fall.

Taking a seat on a stone bench that must become the enclosure for a flower bed in the summer, I try to imagine the feeling of swimming here when I was a boy, but once again my ghosts are gone. One needn't visit a graveyard to conjure the presence of the dead, who are everywhere around us—everywhere...and no where.

Lost in a reverie of introspection, I don't immediately register the sound of footsteps near me until I hear the voice that goes with them.

"Not a day for a dip," Lee says as I look up. The other guests must have left, I realize, as he stands before me. "Come on," he continues. "I'm sure you'd like to see the studio."

"That would be great," I reply. "I was just thinking, seeing the pool even though there is no water…at home, when I go to the college gym, there used to be a short man with thinning hair who'd appear wearing a bathrobe. He's do some stretches, supervised by a trainer I know, and then he'd take the elevator downstairs one flight, where the pool was, and swim several laps. I don't know why this didn't occur to me before, but from your story about Madame Oppenheim and what I remember overhearing about the sweet, elderly man in the robe—how he used to teach at the university, his wife was the daughter of a man who was once a rabbi in Princeton…could he have been Madame Oppenheim's surviving son?"

"It's very likely," says Lee. "She lived a long life, and she'd visit here from time to time. Felix—that was the son's name—came occasionally as well. The woman he was married to was Shulamith, whose father was indeed once a rabbi, and I know she grew up in Princeton."

"Shulamith, yes, that's it. She's still a figure in Amherst. Helps out with the blood bank. Writes children's books. I believe she still lives in the same house where she and Felix raised their family. How amazing."

Suddenly it is Lee who seems someplace else in his thoughts. Saying nothing further, I wait. Finally, he speaks.

"What a striking woman she was, Madame Oppenheim. Gabrielle—that was her first name. How nervous I was that first time, here I was a freshman at Princeton, this would have been in the autumn of 1954, and I'd asked my English professor if he could recommend someone who might help me with this stutter I'd had for nearly half my life. 'It's hopeless,' he said, and then he said there was a woman he'd heard about, a speech therapist from Belgium who'd settled in Princeton with her husband, he had no idea if she could do anything for me. Didn't know her phone number but he gave me her name and told me where she lived, down past the eating clubs around a corner at fifty-seven Princeton Street, an address and a house I will never forget."

Gabrielle Oppenheim's house, Princeton, N. J.

We've reached the former studio now, in a wooded area beyond the part of the driveway that is behind the house. Stopping near a window, Lee pauses again before resuming his story.

"She took me on. I would come to her house and she would have me lie on a blue couch in a small room that was also blue. It even had blue curtains. And I would lie there on that couch and read aloud passages from racy novels by D.H. Lawrence, *Sons and Lovers* and *Lady Chatterley's Lover,* which was still considered scandalous back then. I became so absorbed in what I was reading…well, more accurately, aroused…that slowly and surely my stutter disappeared. It was a miracle.

"And then something else happened that also changed my life. Every Saturday, Gabrielle invited special guests to partake in a salon. Einstein used to come, in fact Einstein was the best man at the wedding of Felix and Shulamith. Einstein died that spring after I started seeing Madame Oppenheim, but I met him, met him at her house.

"How it happened was that to be invited to the salon you had to speak at least one language other than English, and from my studies and then my travels the summer after my junior year in high school I was fairly fluent in French. But I think it was something else, too, as if I were becoming the surrogate of the son she had lost in that terrible tragedy, the Cocoanut Grove fire in Boston. I also looked like him."

We're looking through the Albert Spalding studio window as Lee says, suddenly changing the subject, "This is where we had our first concerts." The couple from Philadelphia who rent it now aren't here this weekend, so Lee's knock on the door goes unanswered. Stepping inside the studio will have to wait for another time. So will further conversation about Madame Oppenheim—I need to be on my way—but Lee's story about her has reminded me of something a musician friend once said to me.

"When something is great, it echoes, and each echo is bigger than what it came from. Think of the sound of a bagpipe in a battle. Or go to the edge of a canyon and shout, 'hello!' The major function of your existence is to do something that will ricochet, like the echo of your voice from that cliff."

Yes, I think to myself, here from high on this hallowed hill…this vibrant voice…echoing far beyond this magic kingdom.

But who is this man?

3. *Friends and Family*

"I believe in the holiness of the heart's affections
and the truth of the imagination."
—Keats

Lee and Judy, September 2011.

Seeking an answer to my question, I ask Lee for the
names of friends and family members with whom I might
speak. The list is a long one, and it includes two former wives,
several past girl friends, and a host of business, professional,
and personal relationships. Their collective comments and rec-
ollections form a kind of salon in which the subject of the
convocation is the man they've worked with or ridden with,
lunched with, climbed with, slept with, lived with.

Judy Ney

I am so lucky! Lee is a superb companion. He has a knockout
sense of humor and enormous knowledge and intelligence,
really a photographic memory. If I mention a play or opera,
he will say something like, "oh, I remember seeing that in
February 1973 in Chicago," and naming the actor or singer.
It really is stunning, this occurs regularly.

Lee is fascinated by words and their origins, as am I,
and so we try and one up each other with obscure words and
their meanings. Lee is hugely energetic and never wants to
stay home unless he is entertaining at lunch or dinner. He
always knows what is playing in theaters all over town and
is curious about much of it. He always sees the bright side
of anything and only the good traits in people. He is not a
worrier and assumes things will work out well. Lee is pretty
much without any kind of fear. Whether physical challenges

or personal or business obstacles, he moves ahead and perseveres. Lee is wonderfully cozy and loves making new friends whenever he meets people. He is also kind and friendly to animals. This man is a true original.

Bob Sullivan

I am a civil engineer. I grew up in the Boston area and was living in Connecticut when I formed an LLC with six other people several years ago. Our idea was to purchase the property of a defunct school in Stockbridge and turn it into a high-end, equestrian themed resort. We had lots of support and about $200 million in financial backing lined up. Then in September of 2008, the recession hit. And we were only three weeks away from filing for our permits.

Lee's name had come up earlier when we were planning our financing. One day in the spring of 2007, when Lee was at his New York office, I made a cold call, soliciting his help.

"Come by my place in Great Barrington at four-thirty this Saturday," Lee said. "We'll talk on the terrace. And then I have to leave for a concert at five-thirty."

When I arrived, there was no one there. Had he forgotten? Did I have the day or time wrong?

Nothing to do but wait. And then, suddenly, Lee appears—on a horse!

I'm thinking we probably have just ten minutes to talk before he has to get ready and then leave for his concert. Instead, we talked for an hour.

"What about your concert?" I asked.

"I'll catch the second act," he answered.

Turns out, he never went.

When I mentioned to him that I also rode horses, he asked me if I were free the next morning. The truth was that I hadn't ridden in at least a year. But of course I said okay.

That night I talked with my wife about what kind of ride I expected it to be, since I figured Lee was probably at least 20 years older than me. The next day, we started out slowly along the highway, crossing the Green River at the bridge, and then took a left up toward Wyantenuck Country Club, where I later learned Lee was a competitive tennis player.

"Shall we canter?" he asked.

"Sure!" I said.

Then, as we started uphill, Lee took off at a full gallop. I raced to keep up.

"How was that?" he exclaimed, smiling, when we'd reached the top of the hill.

"Fantastic," I said.

Lee turned to the other two men in our group and announced, "He can ride with us."

That was the beginning of our friendship. I live in the Berkshires now, and we still ride together frequently. It's not so much the length of the rides that amazes me as the kind of terrain Lee will choose. He'll find a field that looks like it's waiting to be galloped across—and off we go! Sometimes it seems to me it's like an English fox hunt, without the fox and dogs and twenty other people.

Lee to me is someone who is completely present in whatever he is doing. And he's able to compartmentalize, and then as soon as he has to he changes gears. There's also a public Lee and a private Lee...he reminds me of the person in those ads for Dos Equis: the most interesting man in the world.

Peter Strauss

We go way back. It must have been the early sixties when we first met—in Paris. Lee was doing some work for the firm of Cleary Gottlieb Steen & Hamilton, and I was an intern. I had a motorcycle back then, and I'd give Lee rides. He was a backseat driver, which is ironic because he must be the world's worst driver! Our friendship continued in New York, where Lee and his first wife Dorothea would invite me for dinner. He was so gracious and welcoming. I went to law school then and afterwards left New York for a few years to run my father's business in Missouri. I returned in 1968 and was in the city for the next ten years, and Lee would invite me for social outings. After he bought Aston Magna I visited there several times. We'd share ideas and thoughts and did a few business things together. I moved to California, but we continued to talk often. And then in 1995 I became a major investor in his real estate transactions and still am. Lee is very bifurcated—he has these different lives but he keeps them separate. He is discreet. Highly intelligent. So well educated. Such an interesting, provocative person.

James Brooke

I've been working for Lee for about a year, but I've known him much longer. He and my father are friends. I'm sure he's read some of my father's books. And there's the Berkshires, where my family has had a home for more than a century. And I was born in Brazil, where Lee once lived, where his first wife Dorothea was from.

He is very intelligent and has a phenomenal memory. He remembers phone numbers from years ago. And he has an amazing ability to handle the pressure of working in a business with a young crowd. We have our computers and logarithms, but Lee does it all by hand, works out these deals, has everything in his head.

It's phenomenal.

Jay Goldin

I've known Lee for years, starting at Princeton, casually, then Yale Law School, where of course I also met his first wife, Dorothea, and then in New York, for about 50 years now. Lee is charming, fun, kind…he'd give me the shirt off his back. When I first ran for comptroller in New York, Dorothea did the designs for all my political brochures and posters.

Charles Goldstein

I met Lee through Jay Goldin, whom I'd known since the early sixties, it must have been in 'sixty-two or 'sixty-three, and when Jay was campaigning—before he was comptroller he was a state senator—that was when I met Lee, at some kind of campaign event.

Lee has always been a man of many parts, a man of unquenchable interest in everything. He takes such an active part in life, in his climbing, his music, in Aston Magna, which is a musical oasis. And I knew Dorothea, vibrant,

Brazilian…it was a good sign that Lee was different from the rest of us. And then many other women who all found him very intelligent and attractive. He makes women feel wanted.

Lee is mature. Literate. And he has faced crises with a great deal of courage. When his daughter lost her sight, that was something that might have crushed others, but he saw it as a challenge and never felt pitied. The fact that she was blind was unspoken. I remember her wedding at Aston Magna, when her groom appeared on a horse.

Lee is someone who is given to dramatic gestures. He's also a chef, runs his business well, and never stops trying at whatever he is doing. He's really like no one else I've ever known, a self-made man who knew what he wanted to become, who wanted to loom large…a great friend who is always there, and someone who never dropped a friend. Self-propelled, Lee created his own mold, from his interests and ambitions…he is a force of nature, who never stops.

We were young lawyers when we met. I remember there was a time when we both had apartments in the same building, and I recall his running up and down the stairs to stay in shape.

What an indomitable spirit! No one has ever put him down, though he is more than some people could handle, because he is so filled with life.

Jane Iredale

I've known Lee at least 25 years, maybe 30, long before I began my cosmetics business, which is here in Great Barrington. We met through a mutual friend, and later I introduced him to some of his lady friends.

I've been to many of his Robert Burns nights and the concerts. And the readings of plays. I remember once we were outside and it started to rain while the actors were reading, and finally someone suggested we'd better go inside, and Lee looked as if he had no idea it was raining!

What energy! Aston Magna is such a magic place. The mix of people. And Lee is so generous.

For someone meeting him now, it's late in the game. He is a whirling dervish.

Mark Hauser

We met through wine—French wine, Burgundy—as fellow members of the Confrérie des Chevaliers du Tastevin. So there were many dinners with wonderful food and wine, and travels to Europe. We've shared many lunches, too, often at his favorite restaurant, Teodora.

Lee is from a different era, a Renaissance character with all the languages he speaks and uses. He can be stubborn. He's really old world, sends handwritten notes, is charming, and his business is based on trust.

I remember a dinner party at my home. We'd invited eight couples. As dessert approached, many of our friends proposed toasts to my wife. Then Lee stood up and recited from memory a poem about friendship and gratitude and hospitality.

He juggles so much, but he prioritizes. Aston Magna is certainly a beautiful property...I can picture Lee outside cooking, his guests wandering around the grounds.

Whatever he might do or say, he gets away with it with his impish grin. One of his great passions, of course, is mountain climbing, and I remember calling recently with Lee on a man in New York on whose apartment walls there were photographs of famous mountains. As he looked at the photos, Lee named each of them.

"Do you still climb?" our host asked Lee.

"Only mons veneris," replied Lee.

"What is that?" said the host.

"The perfect slope," said Lee.

Felipe Propper

I've been with Morgan Stanley and its predecessors since 1955, and I've known Lee Elman for about 30 years. We've been to several concerts together and I've visited Aston Magna. Few things deter him, and he's a good consultant on what to see and hear. We'll meet for lunch, and mostly what we discuss are serious matters—politics, business, investments. He'll tell a joke or share an anecdote, which is always anything but boring. He is a very loyal man, my friend Lee, whom I place on an informal but very deserved pedestal.

Fritz Selby

Lee Elman is enthusiastic about whatever he gets into, and he is a fast learner. In the time I've known him, he has taken up horsemanship. What Lee did is he learned how to saddle a horse, and so many of the technicalities that there are with horses.

I give him a lot of credit, because a lot of people sit on their rear ends and don't do much and he goes out and he does it. I know he used to ski. I went cross-country skiing with him up in the Adirondacks. He gives it his all…he's game for almost anything, as long as he has at least a bit of knowledge about it, and then he tries to learn more. He does the same thing intellectually, talking about certain writers, literature, music, or languages…he tries to get more knowledge, because he's interested and he wants to be proficient. That's a great characteristic.

Lee and I first met socially. We might have met at Aspen, through a fellow who was a Broadway producer, I believe, and then we got together many, many times. I enjoy his company. I actually have him down in a codicil to my will as giving a eulogy at my funeral. That's how much I think of him. I've never had a boring moment with Lee, because Lee is so interested in everything and is interesting. He's not one-sided. He's multi-faceted. When people too often use the term Renaissance man, I don't know what else you could call him, because he really is. I wish there were another name for it.

Here he is, he knows his classical music, and he loves it. He doesn't go to concerts or operas because it's the thing to do. He goes because he loves the music. He yells and screams at the end of it, because he's terribly enthusiastic. Same thing about the theater; he's a real patron of the arts. He's out every night.

We are similar in our outlooks in the political world. We discuss current events. We discuss court cases. We discuss whatever is the subject of the day. People we know.

He looks at people very favorably, always. He looks at the best in people. Lee is relatively never negative about anybody. He's almost like a babe in the woods when it comes to certain individuals, including women. He meets someone and is enthusiastic and it takes him a long time to lose that enthusiasm. He just looks for the best in people. He is positive.

Lee is basically self-made. He talks a lot about his mother, but he rarely talks about his father. Due to his closeness with his mother, he's very female oriented, more so than most men. He almost feels like he needs the company of women to go out. He praises them and puts them on something of a pedestal. It's very hard for him to become negative about a woman. To him, a woman is terrific. He retains the image of a goddess in a woman. I don't know of any other of my male friends who are that way about women. Sex is only one aspect of this.

A friend of mine, a lady, gives a major cocktail party every year for a cast of hundreds of fairly socially prominent people in the upper East Side. One time she needed some extra men, so I asked Lee if he'd like to be invited, and he said, "yes, of course." I gave the hostess Lee's address and she invited him. And he brings a woman. He was not asked to bring a woman. But to him it is automatic that for an evening to be worthwhile, you bring a woman.

Lee is happiest when he is in a relationship. In the time I've known him he's had ten girl friends.

He's a good father. You have to admire him for that. It's good to see.

He also happens to be if not the best, one of the best hosts I've ever encountered, and not just because he gives parties and loves parties. He truly wants his guests to enjoy themselves. He watches over every detail, whether it's the wine or the food or the seating...the environment, the atmosphere. He's just a superb host. His heart is in it. He wants you to feel that you've had a lovely evening or luncheon, whatever, with him. He's a giving person, which is also one of the reasons women like him. He makes them feel wanted. He's complimentary—"you look good," "you look marvelous."

A lot of his business transactions are very difficult. He has to raise the money. He has a limited period of time and must constantly wonder who the investors are going to be, which bank is going to do the debt and on what terms.

In order to have buildings under contract, you've got to get the owner of the building to sell to you. Why should he sell to you? First, because he feels you are going to operate that building in a first class manner, that the tenants will be well served; number two, that you'll give him the right price; and three, that the price is going to be based on a number of payouts on which you are going to be good on your word, that you have the right backing...there are a number of factors.

In Lee's case, you also have to have a relationship with the U.S. government. Who's going to call you from Washington and say, "We're looking for a building in Wichita, Kansas, for Social Security?" Not everybody has that relationship, not everybody knows where to get the money—who is interested in investing in that kind of a building.

Something I will never forget: Lee rented a van to take his horses to a hunter pace event in Connecticut. This was about ten years ago.

It was the kind of event where you have to wear the right kind of tie, you have to have a certain stick pin, the right kind of a coat, the right color, the right kind of hat and so forth. There are two places in New York that sell all this finery.

I would think that the average person who gets into this kind of thing has an annual income of at least $250,000 to a million dollars or above. This is not a world of pipers.

So, Lee goes and gets all the right kind of clothing. And he gets the van. And he's going to this event in Connecticut that starts early in the morning and then has what they call a hunt breakfast, but it's really lunch, which is very social, with everybody meeting one another in their riding clothes.

The weekend of the event, Lee gets up early. When you get there, every person has a time. There is an order, and you must be on the starting line when they announce your name. "Mr. Elman, you are starting in five minutes. Mr. Elman, are you here?" And so it goes, until everyone is off on these jumps. Often it's two people who go as a pair, and it's the combined time of the pair that counts.

Lee asked me the night before if I minded if he woke me up early to make sure he looked okay.

"Absolutely," I said. "Please do. What time will you wake me?"

"Six o'clock."

"That's fine."

So, that morning, Lee wakes me, and I help him get ready. He looks marvelous.

"When will I see you?" I asked.

"Oh, I suppose sometime in the afternoon."

"Fine, take your time. Enjoy yourself. Good luck."

I then went back to bed. About eight o'clock, I woke up again and walked to the kitchen to make myself some coffee and eat some toast. Lee is sitting there, still in his regalia.

"Lee," I said, "what's...what's going on ?"

"I couldn't get the horse into the van."

He hadn't wanted to wake me again.

There's a way of getting a horse in a van. It's not a pretty thing. You put on a glove and stick your hand in the horse's rear-end and there he goes into the van. Pushing is not going to do it.

He was stoic about it. He sat there in the kitchen, reading the paper.

Another incident that sticks in my mind: in 2003, we went up to Kilimanjaro. It's basically an altitude trek. There's nothing technical involved. It's an uphill hike.

There were ten of us, men and women. I like people when I do something like this to learn something about where they're going. What is the history of Tanzania? When was this mountain first climbed? What were the circumstances? We were on safari, so what is the history of safaris?

I wrote up a summary for people to read and prepared a test of 10 or 12 questions. Before the trip, I mailed the summary to everyone and said we'd have the test the night before we left. And I bought a bottle of good champagne for the person did the best on the test.

Two people never read my summary and handed in no answers. Lee won the contest. I knew he would. I knew he would study the summary. He was interested in the material. And he likes to win tests. He's not someone who goes through his life with his eyes closed. He wants to know what is going on in the world. When he found out the history of safaris, that the word is Swahili for journey, he was interested. And so he won the champagne.

Now, we get up to the mountain—it's about 19,200 feet high—and we're at about 12,000. And we're heading on loose pebbles along a dry path, which is very dangerous, because the pebbles roll and you have no stability for your feet.

Lee was back behind me, chatting away with someone. All of a sudden, I heard a scream, and Lee went down. I waited a minute to see what happened—we were spread out—as Lee tried to get up, and then went down again.

One of the guides took Lee on his back and carried him a half mile or so to the place where we had been camping. It appeared that Lee might have broken his ankle, which meant that the trip was over for him.

We had extra guides and porters, and they wanted to make a stretcher for him. Lee didn't want to be carried down the mountain. He wanted to be helicoptered. By cellphone, we found a helicopter in Kenya, which said it would come the following morning and we were to mark the place where we were.

"How should we mark it?" I asked.

"With a white circle," I was told.

The only thing I could think to do was take toilet paper and make a huge circle with stones on it. In the meantime, we made up a little splint for Lee. He smiled, didn't complain…he was stoic about it. He didn't cry, "why did it have to be me?"

At eight o'clock the next morning we heard whirring overhead. There had never been helicopter rescue on Kilimanjaro.

"Is that toilet paper down there," the pilot shouted. "You better gather it up, so it isn't sucked up into the engine."

Finally, the helicopter lands. We take Lee under his arms and he uses his one good foot to get in.

I was very sad about what happened. I had wanted to be on the summit with him. It would have been a nice gesture for two friends. He would have made it easily. Instead, he was taken to a hospital, where they put a pin in his ankle. Then he was taken to an airport, and he flew home to New York.

He never complained.

Another time, it was a beautiful day to summit Monte Rosa, the highest mountain in Switzerland. And so we were in a shelter, sleeping, I suppose at around 10,000 feet. In the morning, the guide woke us up very early, because climbing starts early, when the snow is firm. And so we started going up with our head-lamps on, and by the time we got to about 13,000 feet I began to feel absolutely rotten.

I had to sit on a rock. The feeling didn't go away. The guide made me go down, and he was the only guide with the three of us. I had ruined the climb for everybody.

Lee never said, "you ruined my day." That to me was such a fine quality, understanding that his friend had a physical problem and the thing to do was to get him down.

Time out. If this oral history, this "festschrift" of Lee, were truly a salon, I can imagine an intermission during which Lee mingles as he pours each guest a glass of wine, asks them something about work or home, a person they both know or a place they've just been to. If the occasion were a formal one, I can see him in white linen pants and a double-breasted blue jacket. But this gathering is more likely to take place outside Aston Magna, late in the afternoon of a summer's day, and for Lee his informal attire includes blue jeans and a checked scarf he has tied around his neck, Clark Gable style.

And I'm trying to count all the people. How can any one person be such a presence in the lives of so many others?

• A poet, Sandra Hochman, to whom he once said, "My life is like a piece that I divide into seven sections. My professional life, my family, my social life, my pro-bono work in the cultural world, my life as a sportsman, and my life at my country home. And then of course there is my private life, my seventh life, with myself, when I walk in the country and spend time alone, in reflection."

• A dear friend from his Yale days, Marie-Monique Steckel, who recalls the summer Lee went salmon fishing in Alaska, "and he gave his entire estate to my husband and me to invite our family from France."

• A longtime and extraordinary supporter of the Aston Magna festival concerts and foundation, and former chairman of the foundation, Robert Strassler, who says, "Not taking no for an answer is one of Lee's greatest qualities."

• Another Yale friend, Crawford Shaw, who remembers when, "Lee and I chipped in $100 together and bought a car which we called Charlie. Charlie took us to some indiscreet and clandestine destinations in the last year of law school."

• Annie Rye, a longtime friend, has written that, "Although Aston Magna has been host to scores of people, it remains a private home. Whether invited guests come for the vineyard, lunch, dinners, riding, swimming, or any of the other assorted events at the estate, they can be guaranteed a unique experience. It's because Aston Magna is more than historic, more than festive, more than just a house; it's a lifestyle."

Standing somewhere in the back, trying once more to keep track of everyone, I can see myself nodding as Lee reminds me again to speak with a close Princeton friend, Norman Peck.

"You have to get hold of him," Lee says, and then repeats Peck's phone numbers—home, business, and cell. He remembers these things, just as he knows the names of his friends' children and even grandchildren. He once pleasantly startled me by quoting a brief passage from something I'd written about a rural town where I used to live, and then he told me how my depiction had reminded him of the Mount Kisco he knew as a boy, long before it became an overgrown suburb of New York.

When I suggested we have a conversation about my visits with his friends, Lee selected a Berkshires date with nothing on his calendar but an early evening recital at one of the mansions in nearby Lenox.

"Come early," he said, "so you can go to the concert with us, and then stay late and I'll make us dinner and open a special wine."

Whether it was in the way he says, "darling," to Judy, the gleam in his eye over a favorite joke, the penetrating focus in his attention at a concert of live music, the energy in his voice when he speaks up at a gathering, his ability to seek out and find the good in others, the complete absence of pomposity or airs, the sharing of his home and its surroundings, the eagerness with which he greets a guest, the compliments he always remembers to make, the elegance of his speech and bearing, the wide range of his learning and reference, the love one sees and feels in every moment with or mention of his daughter, the skill with which he navigates the high stakes of his business, the modesty with which he describes such, his recall of detail whether from years ago (meeting Madame Oppenheim) or last week (attending a new play), his calm at moments of high stress (finalizing a deal, looking for horses on the loose), his patient attention when someone takes longer than she or he should to get to some point, his refusal to gossip or say a bad word about another person, his refusal to let disappointment deter him, his determination always to stay in the present, to affirm what is most important in life even as he grasps the fleeting nature and mystery of so much of our existence...all this had come to define a grace and gift that was leading me to think of him as a kind of beneficent Merlin, the magician of a domain that knew no impediment or border save that of our mutual mortal coil.

I had recently stumbled on a Hemingway biography I hadn't read. It was the thesis of the biography's author that Hemingway's great achievement was transmuting (my shorthand verb) his anxieties into art. Much of the book, which I skimmed, traversed the great writer's many mood swings. This got me thinking in a new way about an epiphany I'd just had that morning, wherein I felt that I finally grasped what I believed was the essence of my own experience with Lee and what all these people he'd put me in touch with were saying, each in his or her own way, in part simply by the mere act of saying.

Several years ago, when I was in the midst of a project with a noted musician, a person who may be closer to him than anyone wrote me, and I paraphrase, that within him and thus within his art there was no polarity, no east nor west. For polarity in Hemingway I read mood. And it dawned on me that perhaps the great "magic" at Aston Magna is that it's not magic at all.

Vineyards in Chianti, 1995.

"No doubt," I wrote Lee, "this is something ideally discussed in person over cognac. Perhaps," I continued, "another way of suggesting the truth is darkness or vulnerability, the quality that to me comes through in all great art."

And he wrote me back: "Yes I have ideas on all the issues which you unearthed and set forth. And I agree that vulnerability is a good antonym, a good yang as opposed to a yin. More on this later. And yes I would be amenable to sharing a good Armagnac with you at Aston Magna or elsewhere. To that point, what are you doing on Sunday? Could you come over? Alternatively, you could join us for a concert of Close Encounters with Music at

Ventfort Hall in Lenox, have Armagnac afterwards at A.M. and stay overnight. How 'bout it?"

When I called to accept, he asked me if I'd seen Jill Spalding yet. "You must!" he said. "She's was a very important person in my life. And she lives in the same building in New York as I do." I was happy to tell him I'd had a long conversation with her, reminding me again that none of us can truly know another person.

Jill Spalding

Lee is very real. He made himself into the person he wanted to be, and Aston Magna is a kind of Valhalla. He has such a largeness of spirit, never says an unkind word about another person, never gossips, never defames someone else's character. I remember a family friend whose nephew caused some kind of scandal. "What are you doing?" Lee asked when his friend seemed to be judging what had happened. "There are always two sides." That was absolutely Lee, and it's never for show. He is simply warm, generous, accepting.

On the other hand, he seems to have a need to chalk up experience. It's almost frantic, as if he were trying to defeat mortality, "to pee on every post," so to speak. It's a kind of classical wanting to be part of history.

Lee is the head of a club of his own construct. We met about twenty years ago, and were together on and off. All sorts of things happened, and there was a bit of drama at the ending.

I was so exhausted. I could not handle it. Racing for the next deal. The pace of his life. We were never home alone just to read the newspaper.

Lee has burned the candle at both ends. There have been stumbles, but he has lived large.

There is not a mean bone in his body. And he is very loyal. Also a little naïve, for example about his health, with all the cigars he smokes and alcohol he drinks.

I can't imagine him taking up meditation. He's not a tranquil sort of soul.

I know what a passion climbing is for him, so whenever I see something in the newspaper, about climbing, even if it's little, I clip it out and leave it for him under the door to his apartment. Same thing with anything about Hemingway.

Norman Peck

Lee Elman has been such an influence on my life. And our meeting was serendipitous.

Lee was a year behind me at Princeton. I was a sophomore, and he lived in a nearby dorm. Princeton was rather isolated back then. No cars for students were allowed. There were no hedge funds with offices in town. It was a quiet, lovely place.

I used to play poker at Princeton. At some point Lee came to watch—he did not play—and we'd chat. Gradually, we became friends and I'd see him now and then.

Meanwhile, my father ran out of money. How was I going to pay for my senior year? Princeton made me a loan, which helped. Then, one day, I went to have a drink with a friend at the Princeton Club in New York.

Waiting outside—I was early—I noticed there was a haberdashery store next door to the club. The store sold very nice ties for $2.50 each. I wondered: could I sell such ties for a profit to my fellow students at Princeton?

After making an inquiry, I called on a payphone and then visited on the lower East side a sweatshop where the ties were made. A holocaust survivor was in charge, and he explained that he made the ties from the remnants of cloth bolts.

I made arrangements to leave school each Friday and pickup ties that I ordered, which I then brought back to Princeton, where I had a group of guys who would then sell the ties door-to-door for $1.50 each. Lee became one of the salesman. Some of my guys sold 100 ties a night, and I would pay them a commission. When I graduated, I picked Lee to run what by then was called the Princeton University Tie Agency.

After graduation, I did my military service, having been in R.O.T.C. during college. When I returned, Lee was in Bologna on his Fulbright. Soon thereafter, however, he was married, and I would see him and his wife Dorothea at Yale. What a great cook she was! They would host dinner parties, where I met many interesting people, including George Soros. After dinner, we'd roll up the rug and dance to recorded music.

Later, after his divorce from Dorothea, I met a French woman through Lee at another party. She eventually became my wife.

Lee is really an anomaly. By all rights, he should just be an intellectual. He is quick. Analytic. He is rational. And compartmentalizes.

He has gotten a little calmer, but he is still so exuberant! He has a compelling need for being with other people. He thrives on it, the energy of it.

People..." I like humanity," a friend once told me. "It's people I can't stand." Another friend said, "don't tell me what you hate. Give me what you love."

Love..." I understand with love," wrote Chekhov, "if you start theorizing about it, you must have a nobler, more meaningful starting point than mere happiness or unhappiness, sin or virtue, as they are commonly understood. Otherwise, it's best not to theorize at all."

Elaine Sargent

I was a widow when we met, and he'd been a bachelor for many years since the end of his first marriage. He was always climbing mountains, going places, doing things. He was truly a Renaissance man, very unusual, a man with no fear. I remember once when he was learning to climb in the back of a barn. I thought he was out riding, but he was inside the barn, climbing up a wall on which he'd hammered very heavy, thick, nails. When I found him there he was way up on that wall, very high in the air.

Another time he wanted to learn how to jump while he was riding his horse, and he took lessons. Then he went to hunter paces. In one of these events there were some kids in his group, and I can still see them returning one day without Lee.

"Can you imagine," one of them said, "that idiot fell off four times, but he kept getting back on and trying again." Finally he showed up, covered in blood.

After I met Lee I invited him to come up to my house in North Salem, north of New York. "If you have your German girl friend with you," I said, "keep her in the trunk and then come inside for a drink."

Then he invited me to Aston Magna. I told him I would only come if my chauffeur drove me. That way I could leave in a hurry if I had to. Turns out he had a door between his bedroom and the guest room. I looked up and there he was.

The only negative thing I could say about Lee was that he never wanted to be alone. But it makes me happy to think about him, to think of all he does, especially with his daughter Alex. What a great father he is to her. Yes, I am very happy for him.

Dorothea Elman Winston

I was studying painting for a year at the Accademia di Belle Arti di Firenze.

One morning, I met a woman, Nina, who was the wife of a Princeton professor named Peter. I began to receive invitations from her for lunch and soon was going to her grandmother's every day.

"A friend is coming to visit," Nina announced about a month after we'd met. "He's a journalist and a former student of Peter's, now studying in Bologna. You will have to meet this man. He would be perfect for you!"

I was blown away by the visitor—what a gorgeous man! He had big blue eyes, and he was so charming.

His name was Lee Elman.

Nina and Peter hosted a fabulous party for Lee. Afterwards, we all walked down the main street toward the river, where we passed a dancing place.

"Let's go dancing," Nina said.

A Brazilian, I was a great dancer. So, it turned out, was Lee. He was one hot potato!

Lee spent the night at the pensione, and the next day he came with Nina to my studio at the academy. That was the beginning of our romance. He looked at my work and asked if he could have one of my paintings.

I liked him a lot, and I went to see him in Bologna. Apparently he was dating like crazy. All the guys where he was staying were horrified when I showed up unannounced, because he was in bed with another woman!

Lee had a Vespa, and the next time we saw one another we began to take trips around the country, learning Italian by traveling and going to different restaurants. We would have picnics of cheese and wine and make love in the grass.

One time we went all the way to Venice on the Vespa. I remember we ate squid in black sauce as an appetizer at a ristorante in Venice. What would we like as our main dish, the waiter asked. "The same thing," we said.

Later in the summer, Lee and I went to Greece.

Today, years later, I remember when Alex had all the operations as she started to lose her sight. There was always such hope…and then sadness afterwards, when she still could not see.

She is such an amazing person. I don't know how she does it. Alex is joyous.

Alex Elman

They don't make people like my father anymore. He created a kind of life that really doesn't exist today. It's like he is the personification of real "social media." His life is a romantic story because he loves people.

He never spoiled me. He made me fight for everything I achieved, including my entrepreneurial spirit. When I told him once that I wanted to go to law school, he said he wouldn't pay for that unless it was clear I really wanted to be a lawyer. So I worked in a law firm for two years…and hated it. He was right.

There have been crises in my father's life, going all the way back to his childhood after the Great Depression. Much of my father comes from his mother, who lived to be 99. His father died much younger. And his sisters, my aunts, all shared a familial trait, which is to *do*.

My father does that, does the right thing. He always gives back. No one could have anything bad to say about him. He is my hero. He gives me hope.

Photo by Maren Vigeland

PART II

Looking Back

4. *Lee's Reflections*

"…to describe men first and foremost as occupying a place, a very considerable place compared with the restricted one which is allotted to them in space, a place on the contrary prolonged past measure—for simultaneously, like giants plunged into the years, they touch epochs that are immensely far apart, separated by the slow accretion of many, many days—in the dimension of Time."

—Proust

First festival concert, June 1973.

I am quite overcome by what others have said about me. What must they have been drinking? I hope it was champagne, my favorite beverage.

Seriously, I am overcome with gratitude to have such people in my life. Who was it who said that a man's greatest wealth is his friends? Whether or not I am worthy to be termed a mensch, I know I am a truly rich man to enjoy the company of such men and women. And I am humbled.

Were I to die tomorrow, I would have no regrets. I have lived a full life, and I am very grateful.

Years ago, after the challenge of my father's financial difficulties and the inspiration of my mother's love and support, I began to fashion a philosophy of life that I continued to define and deepen as I grew older. I was lucky to have the benefit of meetings with several artists whose words both inspired and helped me on my way.

As a young man, I drank bourbon with William Faulkner. Over a lifetime's engagement with the theater, I've met many actors and playwrights, including A.R. Gurney, who lives not far from Aston Magna in northwestern Connecticut. Several times, I have made the pilgrimage to New Orleans for the annual Tennessee Williams Literary Festival. I once had the honor of interviewing the Russian poet Yevgeny Yevtushenko.

With Russian poet Yevgeny Yevtushenko, Moscow, July 2002.

On a special occasion in Paris I enjoyed a luncheon with Marie-Madeleine Lioux, a concert pianist and the widow of the French author and statesman Andre Malraux.

With Madame Malraux, widow of Andre Malraux, June 2005 in Passy, Paris.

At the end of this book, I recount several encounters I had with the greatest writer I was honored to meet, Ernest Hemingway, someone whose life and work I have continued to study. What I learned from him and so many of my other artistic encounters is that existence precedes essence, that for a person's life to be meaningful each of us must create that meaning.

In my own experience, attending as many as 70 to 80 plays each year, the theater has been the most critical to me, in my opinion best reflecting the human condition. But all the arts do this. I read voraciously, across all genres—though not as avidly with fiction—and, certainly, music continues to be especially significant to me. Counting the Aston Magna concerts I am privileged to help support, I annually take in more than 100 music events per year.

I've also been something of a cineaste, or cinephile, for as long as I can remember. Judy and I rarely miss a chance to catch the latest opening, though we're more likely to see a foreign film or new drama than another commercial blockbuster. At the recommendation of a friend I saw *The Great Beauty* on my own and liked it so much I took Judy the next night. And I was a big supporter of *Brokeback Mountain*, helping the composer of the subsequent opera to find his financing.

But to return to the beginning, already during my boyhood in Mount Kisco I was discovering principles that have stayed with my ever since. To be successful and happy, we all must learn to be comfortable in our own skin, and for me that has always meant being truthful to oneself and to others.

I'm not perfect—I've never known or heard of anyone who was—but when I promise someone I will do something, whether in my personal or business life, I try to do it.

Over my long career, which has brought our company to its current standing as number one in the country in the niche of buying office buildings leased to the United States government, I've signed hundreds of leases and partnership contracts. Except to refresh myself on some technicality germane to a question, I've never wasted a minute to review the basis of a contract when it came to keeping my word or believing in such for the opposite party. The proverbial handshake and the look in someone's eyes are the only things that should matter.

For me, this belief goes all the way back to the landscaping business I ran in high school, the tennis team I started and then played on, the many languages I studied. I never quarreled with a neighbor about the charge for cutting a lawn. If my opponent's serve just nicked the line to make it good, I didn't pretend it was out, even if such a call were the difference between winning and losing a match. When there were difficult conjugations or moods to master in advanced French, I didn't fake it the next day by saying I'd lost my homework or wasn't feeling well.

I didn't do this to be some sort of Goody Two-shoes, and it's the same for me now, talking with the man who for years has taken care of the Aston Magna grounds, Pete Gagne (who lives in a house adjacent to the estate), about a problem we need to solve with the some trees in the Aston

Magna orchard. "Do the right thing," as my mother taught me, "and not only will you feel better about yourself but so will those around you."

This maxim has stood me in good stead in an extended variety of pro-bono involvements and commitments. Back in the late 1970s, New York mayor Abraham Beame asked me to serve on the board of the city's Commission of Cultural Affairs.

"Thank you, I'd love to," I said. "But I don't want to be a figurehead for good works. I want to be involved."

Those were heady days in a city I've always thought of as the arts capital of the world. Sondheim's terrific *Sundays in the Park With George* premiered. The New York Philharmonic was in the beginning of a long association with music director Zubin Mehta. In 1982, the year before he died, New York City Ballet director George Balanchine presented a festival commemorating the 100th anniversary of Igor Stravinsky's birth.

Looking back, I realize that appointment had as much to do with politics as arts, but I'm fine with that. I have for the most part always been socially a liberal and fiscally a conservative, usually voting Democrat but respecting both sides of the proverbial aisle. Though I understand the origin of today's bipartisanship, I strive to keep an open mind, and my political friendships reflect this.

With Alex and President Carter in the Oval Office, February 1977.

With Mayor Rudolf Giuliani in New York, 2003.

With President and Mrs. Bush at White House after the Kennedy Center Honors, December 2006.

In the midst of my association with the Cultural Commission of the City of New York, I also became a member of the Board of Directors of the New York State Council on the Arts (NYSCA). I continued serving on the city's commission—for 11 years, it turned out—while my work with the NYSCA lasted more than two decades (21 years, to be exact). Through that latter association, and during that period of time, I made a friendship which continues to have an impact on my life, alas now only in memory.

With Nancy Reagan, Metropolitan Museum of Art in New York, March 1985.

Kitty Carlisle Hart already had made a name for herself in many roles as an actress, singer, widow of playwright and Broadway producer Moss Hart, and panelist on television's "To Tell the Truth," when in 1976 Hugh Carey, recently elected governor of New York State, appointed her to the Council on the Arts, on which she was then made chair—a position she held until 1996. Imagine, she was 66 years old when she began her service and 86 when she stepped down! And she lived another remarkable ten years after that.

Beautiful, witty, caring, endearing…how can I begin to describe this woman with whom upon meeting I was immediately taken and am still, more than a decade since her death at age 96. Her portrait hangs on the wall in an Aston Magna bedroom that I still think of as hers, from the many joyful visits she made over the three decades of a romance that knew no sex but deep spiritual intimacy and personal affection. In 1991, when she received the National Medals of Arts from President George H.W. Bush, I was her escort at the Kennedy Center in Washington, D.C. More than once, she confided in me that had she only been born a generation later, or me earlier, "we could have have made great music together."

With Kitty Carlisle Hart at Aston Magna, 1986.

I suppose on the one hand that any intelligent person could question the ideal of perfection. And then on the other hand I might conjecture that any willing union between two adults—in my case, man and woman, but I bless all association of whatever variation, as long as they are consensual—any relationship, whether for one night only or lasting an entire lifetime, carries within itself the prospect if not the presumption of a kind of perfection. Why else, I have often said to myself, are we to court one another?

Yes, yes, I know. Heavens, I more than know.

And yet, if I may confess, I also know—have known, and know still—a bliss, a rapture, in the feeling for another person that today prompts me to question the very ethos of what's commonly referred to as fidelity. Fidelity to what? And for what?

I pledge mine to the beauty of an embrace, the delight of a kiss, the ecstasy of a coupling…to the glory of a naked twosome one afternoon by the river down the hill from my Great Barrington estate, to other afternoons and nights—and mornings—in each and every room in that venerable house, even the closets and wine cellar, the pool, the guest house, and the stable, too…what bliss!

Neither man nor woman, of course, can live by love alone. And so for many reasons, related and otherwise, I've put myself in new positions that in case after case have led me to fresh enthusiasms, pastimes, and passions. I've already mentioned tennis, which I continued to play competitively until a back injury forced me first to give up singles and then, after another surgery, doubles. But I'll still spend an hour now and then, rallying with the pro at the Wyantenuck Country Club in Great Barrington. And I always tune in the Grand Slam events on television if I'm free—and, by the way, other than DVDs, that's pretty much the only television I ever watch.

Likewise, downhill skiing in the Berkshires and elsewhere was a big part of my recreational—and paternal—life until just recently. Before she lost her sight, Alex and I were regulars at Great Barrington's Butternut ski area, a homey, family area that despite its small size has won many accolades. And my daughter and I used to fly west, skiing such resorts as Aspen, Colorado, and Alta, Utah, in the type of deep powder that I initially learned to handle as a young man in the Italian, French, and Swiss Alps.

Elsewhere in this book, the dual, central roles that horseback riding every weekend and mountain climbing on five continents have played in my sporting life are well documented. I would be remiss not to include here a few of my favorite photos from these defining experiences.

More than one of my close friends has asked me about the risks and rewards of activities that, I suppose in the way I went at them, might also strike those same friends as obsessions.

To such inquiries, no doubt well meant, I respond that life itself is dangerous, and we never know when it will end, only that it will.

My regular riding group in the summer of 2010.

With Banner during the winter of 2010-2011.

At the Millbrook Hunter Pace, in October 2003.

Three that didn't get away in Rio de Janeiro, 1988.

*At the top of a dormant volcano,
Cotopaxi, Equador, 1993.*

In the Adirondacks, 1990.

Monte Rosa, Switzerland,
July 1989.

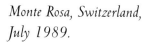

With Sir Edmund Hilary, one
of the first two men to climb
to the summit of Mt. Everest,
San Francisco, circa 1992.

Finsteraarhorn,
Switzerland, July 1988.

At Aston Magna with Chuck Yeager and American climber John Roskelley in September 1986 (just after climbing up to the North Col of Mt. Everest).

With David Breashears, first American to reach summit of Mt. Everest twice, at annual dinner of American Alpine Club in San Francisco, 2004.

"It's later than you think," I find myself repeating, often as not to myself, as well as with whomever I may happen to be enjoying a good cigar or a glass of the wine that Alex's business imports. Those indulgences or pleasures are also passions—I bring home my favorite Cubans whenever I travel abroad, and I've had an oenophile's taste for good wine longer than I can remember. But they are neither fetishes nor affectations, in fact I dislike evidence of any such addictive or phony behavior in people.

Back when Alex was a little girl, about the only restaurant in Great Barrington was Friendly's, an ice cream and hamburger chain. So that's where we went, until eventually we became tired of it.

"What to do?" I asked myself.

"I will learn to cook," I answered.

A father's joy.

And learn I did. I was divorced from my first wife, Alex's mother Dorothea, and so I focused on what a bachelor could cook on weekends in the country for his daughter and his friends.

Back in the city during the work week, I never cooked, not even a late-night snack! But at Aston Magna I found cooking to be both a release from the pressure of work and a pleasure in and of itself.

Eventually I collected all my recipes and menus and with the help of a writer, Gail Steves, published a book, *Country Weekend Cooking*, which is now in its sixth printing.

The Spalding Family salutes Lee Elman, the gracious host of Aston Magna, who carries on and creatively extends the horticultural and gastronomical traditions established there by Mary and Albert Spalding in the 1930s and 1940s.

**Three of Albert Spalding's
Favorite Summer Menus**

Proscuitto e finchi o melone
Blue Crab Newburg*   Tossed Green Salad
Sliced white Georgia Peaches with Whipped Cream

Kedgeree*
Aspargus with Drawn Butter and Parmesan Cheese
Amaretti   Prune Whip*

Cold Mussel or Clam Soup*
Gnocchi alla Romana*
Sliced Tomato and Basil
Raspberry Ring with Fresh Berries and Cream*

* Designates recipes included in this book.

Combing my new discovery of cooking with my ever growing appreciation of wine and my old love of Italy, in 1984 I did something I'd always dreamed of and returned to Italy (where I'd studied and met my first wife) and bought a vineyard. It was called Le Miccine, and it was located in Chianti, where it produced a very fine Chianti Classico. I owned this gorgeous spot, which I visited regularly, for 12 years, selling it regretfully in 1996. But all good things, as I've always known, come to an end.

Lee's estate in Tuscany, Le Miccine, which produced Chianti Classico, ca. June 1986.

Perhaps it was in my genes. Long before I bought Albert Spalding's home, not only had I been exposed to great music since childhood, but my great uncle, Mischa Elman, was himself a violin virtuoso. If only I'd done better with my piano lessons!

When I look at pictures of myself as a boy, I don't see a future Horowitz. But I do recognize someone who will one day hear in the music he listens to the abiding feeling for life—the fervor for experience—that my childhood left me with. And in my mind's ear, whenever I look at the photo of my sister Nina and me dancing on the stage of Tanglewood, I can hear the song that was being played.

Childhood visit to Atlantic City, March 1943 (my sister Nina is about to go overseas with USO; the baby is my sister Jacqueline).

Who can explain the mystery of music, its ability to speak to us in a language that uses no words? Berlioz once asked, at the end of his monumental memoir: what is greater, music or love? Why ask? he continued, "they are twin wings of the soul."

Throughout my life, music has played a very important role in my growth as a person and in my relationships with

Dancing with Nina on stage at Tanglewood in 1972.

others. Always a champion of new music, I have met and in some cases entertained some of the most notable musicians of our time, and I have made frequent travels to enjoy music in faraway places.

Certainly, that now legendary Aston Magna Music Festival—commencing its 43rd season in 2015—is what anyone who knows me will cite as the most well known part of my musical life. And they are right, though the reasons go back a long way and are not just musical but personal.

I was a young man, only in my mid-30s, when the festival began, just a year after I had purchased Aston Magna. Married, the father of an infant girl, with Elman Investors

With Placido Domingo, May 2001 in New York City.

With Judy, my fellow Wagner enthusiast, at Bayreuth in August 2010.

still on the horizon a few years into the future, I was very much living by the existential philosophy I've described. I didn't just want to attend great artistic and social events, I wanted to host them. And I knew for that to transpire, I had to make it happen. And so I did [see photo on page 69].

Now and then, driving back from the Berkshires to New York, I will take a little detour and stop in Mount Kisco. Though the town has grown tremendously since I was a boy, it still has the look and feel of my childhood, and the Elman family house still stands on Beverly Road, just a short distance from the exit on the Saw Mill River Parkway.

I don't know who lives there now, nor would I stop to ask. And someone else runs what was once the family business, though our name has been retained, which you can still make out in the faded letters on an overhead sign out front.

Like Yeats advising fabled horsemen, I pass by. We will all of us now living soon be dust, but I don't let this realization get me down. As long as I am breathing, there is no time for melancholy. Let others weep their nostalgic tears. I am sustained by the light in Judy's eye when we dine together after the opera, by the music in my daughter's voice when she calls to tell me about a new business deal or boyfriend—or to laugh at one another's risqué jokes.

By the complicated succession plan I have devised, Alex will inherit Aston Magna, but I expect she will have to sell it to support her care. Perhaps the new owner will undertake renovations. Will he or she keep the piano in the corner of the main living room, where three quarters of a century ago

Albert Spalding sometimes played four-handed piano music with one of his rehearsal pianists? Will the marble coping around the swimming pool be replaced? Will my network of trails through the woods be kept open or without regular pruning will they grow in?

Who knows?

I do hope the view remains. It has been a comfort and an inspiration to me more moments than I can count: after Patricia died; when I realized Alex would never regain her sight; thinking about a woman in Brazil I loved, or another in New York, still.

I look out.

I listen.

"Heard melodies," wrote Keats, "are sweet, but those unheard are sweeter; therefore, ye soft pipes, play on."

I step outside.

How bracing the night air! Is it autumn or spring?

Foolish question.

At Aston Magna there is but one season.

The present.

PART III
Looking Out

Photo by Maren Vigeland

5. *A Luminous Life*

"Heap we these coppered hulls
With headed poppies
And garlic longed for by the eager dead.

Keep we with sun-caught sails
The westward ocean
Raise we that island on the sea at last

Steep to the gull-less shore
Across the sea rush
Trade we our cargoes with the dead for sleep."

—Archibald MacLeish

Pool, Aston Magna 2013.

Y ou've got mail.

June 12

Please come to a reception at the house after the concert on the 22nd. I am not doing anything this weekend if you'd like to stop by to chat.

June 13

Thank you, I will look forward to that. About the weekend, would Saturday or Sunday morning be better? I'd like to know more about the provenance of the house and improvements you have made and discuss further the beginnings of the concert series. More profoundly, how did you come to believe in the wisdom of that Latin inscription, long before—I suspect—the moment when you discovered the altar that now stands by your pool? I'm sure it must have grown from great conviction, schooled I am guessing during multiple moments when you were prompted to make this decision rather than that, so to speak. Who were you to be doing so in the first place and why, then, did you do what you did? Why, to be more specific, should someone choose to be kind rather than cutting, gracious rather than selfish? How does someone search for and find romance in the face of...of what? I'm sure there was more than a little adversity, there would have to have been. What, colloquially, would be your definition of success in the sense of what Proust called "les intermittences du coeur?"

June 14

Ok to talk mid to late sat or Sun morning. You can stay with us overnight if you wish. However, reserve your seat at the Daniel Center at Simons Rock. The reception is after the concert. See you then.

June 15

Thanks.

This weekend, then, let's plan on that conversation Sunday morning—let me know the time—and then the following weekend I will look forward to the concert and reception.

June 15

Okay, but we have to leave around 3:30 for New York. Also, I recommend we meet at 11:30, but come earlier if you wish for a swim or whatever.

Is that ok with you?

It was more than okay. And so, as if I were borrowing the camera he was always using to take photographs of his guests, I began to focus and then refocus on the mystery that had only deepened since our first meeting and continued throughout my many conversations with his friends, his former wives, some of his girl friends, and his dear daughter, whom I soon realized had inherited not only her father's intelligence but also his sense of humor.

Humor: how to describe Lee's without quoting one of his frequent jokes, typically told with an attention to detail and a tone of deadpan timing that would make Johnny Carson proud.

"So this lady in a fur coat is walking along Park Avenue one cold winter morning," Lee says with a straight face, as if he were describing the origins of one of his real estate deals. The only hint of what's coming is the glint in his bright eyes.

"A person, some kind of activist, comes up to her and asks, 'Do you know how many animals were killed to make the fur for that coat?'"

A pause before the punch line: "'Do you know how many animals I had to sleep with to get this coat?' she says."

Lee's laughter continues with a confession: a few years ago, on his first date with Judy—whom he met through her lawyer, Jeffrey Cohen, also a mountain climbing friend of Lee's—he told her this joke during dinner, only to learn she was on the board of trustees of the Humane Society of the United States.

The good-natured banter between Lee and Judy often turns on the irony that he is a longtime liberal and she is deeply conservative. At one of their summer parties—I missed this one—Judy was stung by a wasp and bitten by a spider, within five minutes. And it seemed so unfair, she thought...she loves animals and is their champion. She was the only one who was stung. Why, Lee wondered rhetorically, was that? And then with a wide smile and great affection, he answered his own

Judy and Lee at the State Department, 2010.

question: "because," he told her, "you are a Republican and this is Berkshire County."

On many other occasions when I was present, Judy would gracefully move in and out of different conversations among the various guests as Lee regaled a friend with another joke —"have you heard the one about the man selling an elephant..."— or inquired about a grandchild, parsed a recent Tanglewood performance, mentioned a new restaurant that had just opened north of town, on the road to Stockbridge.

Food, in fact, was not only expertly prepared and resplendently served, but is also a frequently discussed subject, especially Lee's relish of offal. He loves all kinds, I learned...

from the Haggis that his longtime friend Carl Black prepares every January 25th (or thereabouts) for a dinner Lee hosts at Aston Magna to commemorate the birthday of the Scottish poet Robert Burns—a dinner that begins with champagne and then during which, instead of wine, the beverage of choice is single-malt Scotch, often a highly prized brand brought by a guest—to the specialty meats such as grilled calf kidney and sweetbreads he cooks himself on an outdoor barbecue.

In New York, as well, Lee is gastronomically attentive, habitually beginning each weekday with breakfast at a place called the Palace, near the corner of 57th Street and Lexington, just a short walk from his apartment on Park Avenue and an even shorter distance to his business headquarters on the 25th floor of a building at 57th and Third.

At the Palace he orders half a grapefruit in the winter and half a cantaloupe in the summer. "Then I might vary between poached eggs," he says, "or scrambled, but only as Billy the waiter does them." Sometimes he may switch to a Western omelet or add an order of bacon or a grilled, sliced croissant. And he always has at least two cups of decaf coffee. Lunch is often right across the street at a cozy Italian restaurant, Teodora, where Lee is such a regular that he is usually seated at "his" table.

Twice a week (Tuesdays and Thursdays), if he's not on the road for business or pleasure, he works out after breakfast at a gym in a building almost adjacent to Teodora. Typically he arrives around 8 a.m. and spends about an hour under the guidance of Derek Leite, with whom he trains "hard"—Leite's adverb—while talking with Leite about a wide range of topics, including romance.

"He's one of a kind," says Leite of Lee. "Everyone at the gym knows him, and he remembers each of them by name. Lee cares," Leite continues, placing great emphasis on that verb. "And he's very physical in his training. Even now, after his surgeries"—three operations on his back—"you can tell he was an athlete."

For a man who once climbed to the North Col of Mount Everest when he was 50 years old, it's perhaps not an unusual identification. Nor is the word as I have come to associate it with Lee a reference simply to physical activities that range from the tennis he began playing in high school to the downhill skiing he used to enjoy with Alex. Lee is also supremely competitive in the best sense of that word. Once, on a summer day when it was especially hot, we were sitting by his pool, talking and enjoying a glass of wine, when he invented a spur-of-the-moment contest for me and three young guests to see who could make the best dive off the board at the other end of the pool. Needless to say, I lost that one, but not before Lee had pretended with great good cheer to give each of our dives a numerical ranking, as if this were the Olympics and one of us would soon be awarded a gold medal.

✻

"You can leave the book in my car," Lee says. It's a summer evening, and gold of a different kind—music by Bach—is the prelude to a party.

For more than 40 years, thanks to Lee's vision, buttressed early on by that of the late Albert Fuller, and the generosity of many people, notably a Boston businessman named Bob Strassler, there has been music under the Aston Magna aegis here in the Berkshires and elsewhere. Tonight's concert is being held at nearby Simons Rock, a so-called early college that is now part of Bard. With Judy, Lee is seated in the center of the second row in a small auditorium in the school's performing arts center. Glamorously attired in white linen pants and a double-breasted blue blazer, he looks so focused, so attentively engaged, that one might mistake his energy and élan for that of the concert's two performers, which include the Aston Magna festival's artistic director, violinist Daniel Stepner. To borrow a word from the vocabulary of Buddhist practice, Lee is completely and happily present.

To judge from all I have seen and heard, it has always been this way in his life, going all the way back to his Mount Kisco childhood. His father's marriage to his mother Mildred was his second, and Lee's two sisters from his father's first marriage were much older and already out of the house, leaving Lee to chart a course through the tribulations of an adolescence that might have overwhelmed someone of less vibrant character and ambition.

With the family business in somewhat of a precarious situation and his father recovering from the nervous breakdown triggered by the business travails, Lee did something as he entered his teens that would be emblematic of how for the rest of his life he would face a challenge. He reflected on the situation, taking stock as it were, and then...he acted.

Beyond his studies and athletics, typical pursuits (along with music lessons for a time), he came to an early realization about the financial means that would be necessary for the life he envisioned. And so, at about the age of 14, he started his own business, mowing lawns and doing basic landscaping for friends and neighbors and, soon thereafter, other people in Mount Kisco who heard about him. The business grew and Lee had to hire classmates to help. By the time he finished his junior year in high school, he had saved enough money to send himself to Europe for the summer.

Here, once again, at the start of a pattern that would later define much of his adult life, accomplishment crossed with fate, in this case preparing him without his knowing it at the time for what would be a pivotal development in two years. Lee had always had an ear for language, coming from an early exposure to music and perhaps as recompense, in part, from his childhood stutter. He excelled in French, though his high school teacher's poor elocution set a bad example. Voila! In Europe, Lee made a conscious effort to work hard on his pronunciation, and when he returned for his senior year he was virtually bilingual. A few months later, after rejections or waitlist placements from his initial college choices, his mother suggested they give Princeton a try. That acceptance and the matriculation which followed led to the momentous occasion of his first meeting during the fall of his freshman year with Madame Oppenheim.

"Of course, with the loss of her older son in the Coconut Grove fire, there may have been other factors that influenced how I became part of Gabby's life," he says. "But I never would have become a regular at the salon—the only student, by the way—were it not for my proficiency in French."

What an experience! Through some of the magnificent paintings the Oppenheims owned, he was exposed to great art. And the extraordinary people he encountered included not only Einstein but J. Robert Oppenheimer and Svetlana Stalin, among many others. Was it any wonder that he would shortly feel comfortable encountering Ernest Hemingway, with a recommendation from his English professor (and Hemingway biographer), Carlos Baker?

Lee sought out other luminaries over the coming years and just plain folk who would visit Aston Magna for literary and dramatic readings and discussions. Some of those events have taken place outdoors—notably a semi-staged reading of *Camino Real* by Tennessee Williams (one of Lee's favorite playwrights), with professional actors Lee hired in New York. But many occur in the relative intimacy of the living room.

Returning to the concert: after the music, at a reception in the lobby, Lee clears up a misunderstanding about the car to which he was earlier referring by teasing me with a reference to what he calls his concert car. And what is that, I ask.

"You'll see," he says, eyes twinkling. And then with Judy he departs.

I follow them outside and then stop at the entrance, from which I watch them as, holding hands, they walk to the far end of the parking lot, where they appear to get into a vehicle I've not seen them in before, a larger, older, regal looking...Rolls Royce.

"And I hardly paid anything for it," Lee will tell me afterwards, narrating a tale about a raffle he'd won out west and how he'd used the proceeds to bargain his way into a deal for the car that he then had to have shipped cross country and for which—it's a 1972—it can be a challenge to get parts, and so he really only uses it for fun, taking it to events such as this evening's or to Tanglewood...thus its appellation.

As he tells this story, we're sitting on the terrace at Aston Magna, amongst Judy and Alex and many friends, and I am trying to imagine what thoughts and feelings must cross his mind and heart, a special challenge in Lee's case because he is less apt to share something personal with words and more likely to make a revelation indirectly with the sound of his laughter at another joke, a look upwards at the full moon as he draws on his cigar, an embrace extended upon the departure of a favorite guest.

✽

"I am buoyed by the overall riches of my life and its small triumphs," Lee once said, catching my ear with buoyed (a word
choice, I think, by a lover of languages) and prompting my
skepticism with small triumphs (false modesty?).

After Princeton and the Fulbright in Italy; after marriage
to Dorothea and law school at Yale; and after moving to
New York, he spent more than a decade there and in Brazil
in a variety of pursuits, ranging from commercial financing
to investment banking to the representation in the United
States of international corporate shareholders. In 1976, he
formed Brastelma, Ltd., a company that represented Brazilian
shareholders in the sale of their companies to American and
European corporations. It was headquartered in São Paulo,
where Lee had an office on the famous Avenida Faria Lima for
two years. But something bigger was brewing. Let's let Lee tell
it in his own words:

"By 1978, the bloom was off the Brazilian rose, and I
returned to the United States to establish a buying office for a
group of savvy older European investors interested in picking
up relatively inexpensive American real estate. After three years,
I decided to go on my own, and in the mid-1980s I focused
on buying single-tenant office buildings leased to first class
corporations and banks on relatively long-term leases."

That breakthrough began when Lee was on a trip to Buffalo, New York, to look at a building a broker had recommended. The property proved to be a disappointment. On the way back to the airport, Lee remarked that he was still interested in finding the right building to invest in.

"Can you describe it?" the broker asked, just as they passed the lower end of the city's Main Street.

"I'd like to buy a building like that one," Lee said, pointing to what was Buffalo's highest structure, the world headquarters of the Marine Midland Bank.

"It's not available," the broker replied.

"Are you certain?" Lee said, and then on a hunch added, "why don't you check."

Sure enough, the building was for sale, and Lee put together a group of investors to purchase it. But this was just the beginning.

"In 1996," he explains, "the concentration or focus of my business was further narrowed to acquiring buildings leased only to the government—both federal and state." Today, Lee Elman Investors Inc. is a leader in the field, ranked first in the United States by Real Capital Analytics in mid-2014. Through various groups of investors he has purchased a total of 81 government-leased buildings (as of December 2014), located in 39 states, the District of Columbia and Brazil.

While the income stream from the leases is steady and reliable, the business requires unusual acumen, both in finding the right properties and then in negotiating the terms of acquisition. A master salesman, Lee leverages his well-earned reputation with various government agencies and combines it with his considerable personal charm and gifts as a communicator to grow his company's portfolio.

With the energy and stamina of a person half his age, he regularly travels around the country and abroad to examine new opportunities. He will fly out west, to California, and if he can arrange the schedule to his liking return that night on a redeye, dozing in his coach seat—he doesn't waste money on first class, and he has a rare ability to fall asleep almost immediately in virtually any setting. After arriving near dawn at one of New York's three commercial airports, he'll take a taxi back to his apartment, sleep for another couple of hours, and be at his office first thing when it opens.

Making this work also requires an important commitment to asset management and maintenance of the buildings. Lee's longtime partner, Harvard-educated John Moss, oversees the staff that handles this part of the operation from an administrative office in Long Island. Moss is also involved in negotiating the extension of leases and the occasional but important expansions that "turbo-charge" the net to investors.

Uniquely suited to play this pivotal role in the company's ongoing success, Moss is more than happy to leave the spotlight shining on Lee, whom he describes as "larger than life," a man who "can't slow down" and feels what Moss calls a "need" to be noticed. Moss, on the other hand, says, "I don't have to be seen."

The partnership of the two men, which took a hiatus when Moss went on what he calls a "sabbatical" for several years in the 1990s, seems to work precisely because they are so different from one another. They are a kind of self-defined "odd couple," with fundamental disagreements about what is and isn't important in life. And yet at their core is a clear ability not only to get along but also, and crucially, to ignore their weaknesses—"If I listened to everything John said, we'd never have done a deal," Lee says—and instead to leverage their strengths.

With Moss keeping an eye on details, Lee has also been able to continue giving back in a variety of venues. He has made several gifts to his alma mater, endowing a scholarship at the Woodrow Wilson School for a junior to do research abroad on his or her senior thesis and creating prizes for outstanding, graduating seniors in both Portuguese and English (the latter is called the Hemingway prize).

Simultaneously, and continuing to the present, Lee has kept his devotion to the Aston Magna Foundation and its annual music festival uppermost in his commitments. He continues to serve on its board and to support it financially. Such past programs as a Summer Academy in Great Barrington for musicians and scholars are no longer held, but in their place the foundation now co-sponsors during the year with Brandeis University workshops in period instruments. The five-week concert series in June and July remains the oldest summer festival devoted to music performed on period instruments in the United States.

Though most of the repertoire comes from music of earlier times, the 42nd festival season in 2014 concluded with a new work by the young contemporary composer Nico Muhly. Entitled "Aston Magna," and based on a clever interweaving of themes representing the different rooms of Lee's estate, the piece was commissioned by Lee in 2012.

No stranger to the avant garde, Lee is in fact passionate about modern music, as comfortable making conversational references to John Cage as to Bach or Mozart. Also an opera devotee—he has seen the complete Ring cycle of Wagner several times, including at Bayreuth—he took Judy on one of their first dates to a Metropolitan Opera production of Strauss's *Der Rosenkavalier*. He even has musical dreams, especially a recurrent one of walking out onto the stage at Tanglewood, wearing a white dinner jacket and taking a seat at the piano as the soloist in one of his favorite works, the fiendishly difficult Third Piano Concerto of the Russian composer Serge Prokofiev.

If, beyond the requisite technique and training, the secret of being such a soloist is the uncanny ability to inhabit the role so fully that it seems second nature, then Lee in his long life has pulled off this feat again and again—though not, he would hasten to point out, at the piano. Rather—and, with becoming modesty, he would be the last person to say this about himself— Lee has been the star of different kind of performance. And he's done it so well, and in such an enormous range of realms, that there is no distinction between the private Lee and the public Lee, the business Lee and the patron Lee, the equestrian Lee and the oenophile Lee, the horticultural Lee, the mountain climber Lee, the father Lee, the friend Lee, the host Lee…the romance of his luminous life is his great art.

"Famous 150 years ago," one of my father's stories began, "Arthur Sullivan made his reputation as the composer of the hugely popular operettas on which he collaborated with librettist W.S. Gilbert. But did you know it was a single song that he wrote mid-career at the deathbed of his brother Fred, a singer, for which he was best known during his lifetime in the late nineteenth century? Hymn-like, the song became a kind of anthem, performed by soloists and choirs alike and still a staple of popular concerts in Sullivan's native Great Britain. With lyrics by a poet whose name I have forgotten, the song sends shivers down my spine, with a mysterious message implicit in its title: *The Lost Chord*."

For months, I've been wanting to share this story with Lee, to inquire if its narrative resonated somehow in his own life.

"In the poem that Sullivan set to music," my father's account continued, "an organist sat at the console and played a chord that seemed to answer profound questions about life and death. Then the chord was gone and the organist, who was narrating the poem, could not find it. A reference to angels prompted the thought that the chord must have come from them."

When I first heard this, I felt certain I knew where it was going. Wondering if, when he was playing the organ, my father ever thought of this story himself, I came to the conclusion that it was actually a parable of his own different, but comparable, experience. After his death, I began to feel otherwise, looking as I always was when I thought about him for my own version of this so-called chord. Could that have been what I "heard" within myself the summer day I failed to find the skinny dippers but happened instead upon the magnificence of Aston Magna and the gracious welcome of its owner?

"Born out of the loss of his brother," my father wrote, "the secret of Sullivan's song linked thematically all the way back to the legendary Pythagoras, whose discovery of the ratios among musical tones led to the theory that the planets move somehow in a pattern called the music of the spheres." That part had to come from some research. Though my father continued to surprise me with his knowledge of arcane facts, there was no way Pythagoras was a part of his mental domain. Plus I was the one who was good in math.

"Developed further by other philosophers, this idea was expounded much later and in greater scope and detail first by Copernicus and then Johannes Kepler. The ideal of universal harmony that took form and grew out of their work must have appealed to Sullivan, for the overwrought lyric of his fabled song turns on the image of a similar striving:

I have sought, but I seek it vainly,
That one lost chord divine,
Which came from the soul of the organ,
And entered into mine."

Despite my intentions, I never had a chance to ask Lee directly what he made of this. But as I reflected upon it over many visits, stretching throughout the summer and into the fall and winter, I became certain—with each new story, each new experience, each new opportunity to speak with him or observe him within another setting or scenario...as all this transpired, I was sure of the "answer" he would give me, that he was in fact giving me, not simply through his words but most importantly through his actions.

There was, for vivid example, the July afternoon when, once again, we were sitting outside on the patio at Aston Magna, just the two of us. We'd enjoyed an early lunch, and Lee and Judy as I recall were going out later, so I'd shortly be leaving myself. Judy, in fact, was just then off hiking somewhere, which had something to do with what was about to happen. It was sunny and warm, but a gentle breeze kept us comfortable.

Suddenly, in the distance, far across the lawn, we both noticed the figure of a person walking towards the hairpin corner of the driveway. For a moment, Lee wondered aloud if it could be Judy, but quickly dismissed the thought when he remembered what she had been wearing. Nor did it seem likely that, were she returning from her hike, she would be walking away from the house.

"It's okay!" Lee hollered impulsively, meaning he didn't mind the trespass of whoever it was. I was of course reminded of my own such moment the year before, but before I'd had a chance to say such, Lee stood up and repeated his shout, this time adding, "but come and say hello!"

Within minutes, sitting across from us, was a young woman, Irina Kareva, whom we learned was originally from Russia, now a citizen of the United States. With a recent Ph.D. in applied mathematics from Arizona State University in Tempe, she was presently living in Boston, where she did research in a cancer lab at a major teaching hospital.

And what was Irina doing this weekend in the Berkshires?

"I'm staying with friends here in Great Barrington," she told us, "while I sing tonight at Tanglewood in a BSO performance of Verdi's Requiem. I'm a member of the chorus."

Minutes later, she was off, with an open invitation from Lee to come again, to feel free to stop for a swim even if no one were here—"I'll tell Pete," Lee said, referring to Pete Gagne. What echo...chord...of his past had Lee heard, perhaps subliminally, that had prompted the way Lee responded to a situation that reminded me of a story his first wife, Dorothea, told me?

"We were going to one of those free concerts at Central Park," she said. "There must have been ten thousand people there. And I said, 'Lee, you don't know half the people you've invited.'"

Or what thought or insight or…chord…flew through his mind one winter Sunday when we were gathered around the hearth in the Aston Magna living room and suddenly a sound like thunder reverberated throughout the house? Had the wind come up, presaging a sudden storm?

"No," Lee knew before Judy or I had guessed what was happening. And he was off, split second, grabbing his weathered leather jacket as he headed for the door. "It must be the horses," he said.

And he was right. As he surmised later, they must have gotten loose because whoever was feeding them earlier had not locked the gate in the pasture by the stable. In short order, they were back in the paddock. Lee never lost his composure, never panicked, blamed no one, seemed impervious to a situation that had rattled Judy and startled me.

Or what of the insignificant but telling moment a month or two later, when we were coming back from a concert to which I'd driven us? Lee's car was in the shop after a mishap—not his fault, though he'd often been the culprit. Thinking I knew a shortcut, I'd taken a wrong turn, and before I realized my mistake we'd gone 10 miles out of our way. Sitting in the back seat, Lee barely registered a response when I apologized for my ineptitude. Though he could get worked up when he sensed something was wrong that he might be able to do something about—a real estate deal at a precarious moment of negotiation, a romance in the balance over a misunderstanding—he paid no heed to a matter over which he had no control. His reaction was the same when I reported that an assistant of financier George Soros, an old friend who had been a visitor to Aston Magna, said Mr. Soros would be unavailable for a telephone interview with me because of what the assistant said were "other commitments." We moved on.

As did Lee just a few years ago, already in what was then a budding relationship with Judy, when a simultaneous romance ended as mysteriously as it had started. Again, I wondered, what sense had prompted his understanding, what "chord" had he perhaps listened for, was certain he heard, and then accepted was irrevocably lost?

As he tells it, the story had its origins in a friendship of his late sister Patricia, who also at one point in her shortened life lived in Brazil. The friend's name was Betty Feffer, and Lee remembered meeting her and knowing she was married to a wealthy Brazilian businessman.

Flash forward to 2009 and Lee is in São Paulo to look at the American Consulate building, which he would end up purchasing for his company. At a dinner, his host suggests he give Betty Feffer a call.

"But she's married," Lee says.

"No, she was. But her husband died."

So Lee calls Betty, who has little if any recollection of their meeting 40 years before. He takes her out for a nice evening and does so again a little later on another São Paulo trip. They are becoming friends.

"Will you visit me in New York?" Lee asks. "And we can drive up to the Berkshires. I know you love music. We can go to Tanglewood."

Betty makes the trip, and the weekend that she and Lee come together to Aston Magna coincides with the date of an Aston Magna concert. One of the works performed is by the English composer Henry Purcell, "Music for a while, shall all your thoughts beguile." The couple is deeply affected by the beauty of both the music and the lyric.

Upon her return to Brazil, Betty invites Lee to visit her in the fall, for a social occasion, not business. Unbeknownst to Lee, she makes special plans that are not unveiled until after Lee's arrival.

With several other guests at Betty's country place—a beautiful setting of 200 acres, with ponds and pastures in the state of São Paulo—Lee is escorted on a path festooned with iconography that includes miniature statues of Buddha. At the end of the path is the entrance to a cave that Betty has had furbished so it can accommodate her party. And an area of the cave has been prepared so musicians she has hired can perform on a kind of stage, in front of which are seats for those in attendance. At the conclusion of the concert that follows, the musicians perform Purcell's "Music for a while."

Lee is overcome. A two-year romance commences.

By the time he tells me the story there is an acceptance that is completely in character with a man who pays no attention to a friend's wrong turn, has no comment upon a report about an interview request rebuffed, moves on immediately from a building in Buffalo that isn't up to its advertised billing…a man who long ago heard and never forgot something he learned from the doyenne of a famous Belgian family, who becomes ensconced in Princeton, New Jersey, where she gave speech therapy lessons to students who included a freshman from the outback of Mount Kisco, New York, with a bad stutter: "'There are three kinds of people,' Lee remembers Madame Oppenheim telling him when, fearful and uncertain about his future, he first came to see her. 'People with no instincts, people with instincts that they don't follow, and people with instincts that they do follow.'"

Within myself, I translated this as people who cannot "hear" (see, feel), people who can but do nothing, and people who can and…live.

"What Gabby shared was a gift, but finally you have to create your own life," Lee says to me at a spring meeting. "And you do so, as Malraux put it, 'between the profusion of the earth and the galaxy of the stars.'"

"The great calamity of my life was my daughter's handicap," Lee tells me. "It was a tragedy of its own kind, but you can't look at it that way. You have to find ways to work through it.

"She had been diagnosed with diabetes years before, when she was only eleven, but it was in her twenties that she began to leak blood into her eyes. Diabetes, I learned, attacks blood vessels that are very narrow, for example those that are in one's kidneys. Or eyes.

"Surgeries are performed to cauterize these vessels. Only twenty percent or so do not work. Hers was in that twenty percent.

"I don't know how she does it. She doesn't read Braille. She uses a computer with voice recognition that can write a message and send it or receive a message and convert it to voice. She travels. She runs her business.

"We are very close, talk about anything and everything. She knows about my ladies...she knows most of them.

"I am so inspired by her. We all have to compartmentalize, to choose 'this,' not 'that,' to make our lives...it is why I call myself an existentialist. But Alex..."

The name lingers on the tongue of this man who speaks all these languages—as does she—this lover of words and women, of music, of good food and fine wine, of travel... hard-nosed business deals...fly fishing in the American and Canadian Rockies (catch and release)... ...the evidence—the accoutrements—of Lee's life lie everywhere here in this house on the hill: two fly rods in the corner of the bathroom of what was originally the master bedroom, now its primo guestroom, with a fireplace and mantel over which are mounted several of the old guns from Lee's collection—yes, he was a hunter, too—and along one entire wall, floor to ceiling bookshelves containing every kind of book about every imaginable aspect of the defining passion of his life: climbing.

We have talked around this subject before, never getting to the nub of it. We have talked about the 13th chime on the clock—a story he relates from one of his Yale Law School professors, wherein something someone says or does (the "13th chime") casts doubt on everything he or she had said or done before; we've talked about the great unrequited love of his life, Kitty Carlisle Hart; he's told me about almost buying the Sol Hurok talent agency and another deal that fell through in which he could have become the owner of Tiffany's—when this happens, as he frequently reminds me, "you go on to the next deal" and then the next and the next; he's discoursed at length about what he means by "operational," a mantra in the way he approaches and conducts not only his business but much of his life, even I've wondered, but not inquired, his love life, given his proclivity for making all kinds of lists—he still updates his calendar by hand, and in a suit jacket pocket keeps a chronology of the various cultural events he has attended or is scheduled to each year—including in the case of women friends an actual scrapbook that resides among others in the living room of his Berkshires home.

Lee has shared the story of his miscalculation on the purchase of a house he once owned in Tuscany—"so it's another $50,000, so what!" said Alex, who was with him on a trip celebrating her 16th birthday—advice in a different context that his late brother-in-law, Albert Bildner, gave him in 1961, when Lee turned down an offer to rent Simone de Beauvoir's former Paris apartment because it was a small amount over his budget (Mr. Bildner, married to Lee's beloved sister Patricia, told him afterwards he would have given him the extra money for an apartment that was so much more beautiful than the one a 25-year-old Lee could afford instead). But perhaps it was this advice that Lee would remember ten years later when he bought Aston Magna on the spot, as soon as he and the real estate agent, a friend, reached the fabled hairpin turn and Lee, stunned by the view, said, "the house is irrelevant," by which he meant it didn't matter what the house may or may not have needed (slate roof repair, it turned out, and a renovation of the dining room): he got out his checkbook then and there and gave the agent a check for the deposit on a property that he says he could not really afford, but he found a way.

Aston Magna: the very words, etymologically, hark back in their Anglo Saxon origins to what can be translated as high place, as if in choosing it all these years ago Lee was taking literal ownership of something that strikes me finally as a metaphor for the ever elusive, ever changing, underlying reason and meaning for our existence.

This list is typed, single-spaced, is four pages long, and includes a notation about the climber's height (five feet, 11 inches) and weight (165 pounds). I've never seen anything like it, beginning as it does with reference to Mount Everest (*Joint American-British Expedition via the North Ridge—Support Team Reached 22,500 feet, just above North Col. Aborted attempt due to avalance danger and severe weather*) and concluding with a single reference to a Canadian mountain that is immediately preceded by a list of all the Grand Tetons, all of which were climbed, and the last of which—Static Peak (Wyoming/11,938 feet)—is dated 2004. That is the latest date in the entire summary, marking it as the final climb of 49 total, though two of that number represent a multiple of rock climbs. Among the most well known peaks that appear are Mount Kenya, Mount Kilimanjaro, Mont Blanc, the Matterhorn (the first substantial climb, in 1963, though there was an earlier, much less ambitious trek up an Italian mountain, Gran Sasso d'Italia, the summer after Lee's junior year at Princeton), Mount Rainier, Mount Shasta, Mount Baker, and Mount Owen. The document carries the disarming heading of "Mountaineering Highlights," as if what it alluded to were a tourist's vacation stops or a movie-lover's alltime favorites. The detail and the range belie the heart-stopping reality that during any number of these "highlights," Lee Elman could have died.

"But I really had only one close call," he tells me. "I was climbing Mount Shasta, and it was a warm day in May. Coming down, the snow at the higher elevations had turned slushy. I was unroped—a mistake, which I quickly realized when I slipped and began to fall. Luckily, I was able to self-arrest—to stop myself— just a few feet before a steep cliff. Had I slipped over the cliff, I would have fallen two thousand feet to my certain death."

This occurred in 1990, long before Lee's first spinal fusion, and he was as he admits "in great shape." It was his back problems that put an end to his climbing; had he not had the surgeries he says he would have been crippled.

Had he ever thought about trying once more, I wondered, knowing he was still a member of both the Explorers Club and the American Alpine Club.

"No," he replied immediately, without a trace of self-pity. "I might get up something, but I would never be able to make it down. And you haven't climbed a mountain unless you've climbed back down."

I wondered what else in his life this philosophy applied to, but the attempt at such an analogy seemed forced. And Lee had told me more than once that if he died today, he would feel he had lived a rich life. Judy, during a New York lunch to which she treated me, brought up the word fearless with reference to Lee, and then she coupled it with joy.

If we were all so lucky, I felt, remembering people I'd met who woke up each morning without an idea how they would approach the day. And then it came to me, as I sipped a glass of an Italian red that Lee had just brought back from a reunion in Italy of Fulbright fellows: he was still climbing, and he always would be...not, of course, any of the mountains on that amazing resume, but heights of a different kind, pinnacles of friendship and hospitality, of grace given and grace received.

Coda

Aconcagua 1988.

One Sunday, on my way again to Tanglewood, I stopped first in Great Barrington to see Lee. I'd emailed ahead to say I was coming and we'd set a time, but when I arrived he'd left a note on an old envelope saying he'd be back in ten minutes. I visited with Judy, who was making lunch, and then walked outside to the patio, where one of Lee's regular riding buddies, Yezid Valdes, was sipping a glass of Sam Adams as he sat by the table.

It was a beautiful day, sunny and warm, and Yezid said they'd had a great ride that morning. Though I'd often heard Lee refer to Yezid as the horse whisperer, I'd only just met him a few weeks before. I knew he was originally from Colombia and lived now in New York City. But I had no idea how he and Lee had first connected. Taking a seat, I asked him to tell me.

"You mean you never heard the story," he said, with an emphasis that was more that of an exclamation than a question. Then, smiling and shaking his head, he recalled the moment with such vivid detail I might have thought it happened yesterday, not seven or eight years ago, the exact number being one of the few things he wasn't certain of.

"I was taking a walk with my girl friend," Yezid began. "We'd just come out of some woods and stopped at a swimming hole on the Green River."

My ears immediately perked up. Was this the same swimming hole I'd been looking for two years earlier on the day I met Lee? I continued to listen.

"Suddenly," Yezid said, "there was a loud noise that I immediately recognized as that of a horse. And then the horse appeared, ridden by a man in very nice riding clothes and wearing a helmet. He didn't see us as he rode on past a clearing and then up another trail."

Now I was certain, from the description, that the place Yezid was referring to was indeed the swimming hole that I'd later learned abutted Lee's property. But when I'd visited it, before getting directions and driving into Aston Magna, the scene had been quietly bucolic—not the case in what Yezid next recalled.

"After a very short time, I again heard the sound of horse hooves, followed by the sight of the same horse. But this time there was no one in the saddle! I knew something must have happened."

And so, as an experienced horseman who'd been around horses since his childhood in Colombia, Yezid immediately set out to find the horse, reasoning that it would then lead him to the missing rider. Up the hill he hiked, following the hoof prints on a trail that eventually took him past a vineyard, across a large lawn by a lovely house, around a hairpin bend in a driveway, and to an old stable nestled between a small pasture and some woods. And there he found the horse.

As Yezid was telling me this story, Judy came outside with sandwiches for him and Lee and a salad for herself—I had eaten earlier—and I realized many more than the ten minutes Lee promised had passed. As if she were reading my mind, Judy said he must have run into someone, and I imagined the scene, Lee on his errand, perhaps striking up a conversation with a stranger, perhaps inviting him or her for lunch...you never knew. A smile came to my lips, and I gazed out across the now familiar view toward Mt. Everett, where on a previous visit Lee had told me there was a hidden meadow to which he and Yezid and their friend and riding companion, Bob Sullivan, had often ridden. If you knew where to look, you could just pick out a part of it. Had I been there, too, I wondered, passed by it with my father as a boy?

"Sweet," I thought. But the sadness was gone. I no longer felt either a need or a desire to look back. And as quickly as the thought crossed my mind it disappeared. Memory was not something out "there," it was "here," within. And so, in my recent, revivifying experience, these were Lee's Berkshires now.

But what had happened to the man on the horse, whom I had of course guessed was Lee.

"I had just finished taking off the saddle and brushing the horse's coat when who should appear in the doorway of the stable but the man I'd seen earlier. He'd fallen off his horse in the woods, but happily I could see he was okay. 'Who are you?' he asked, and I told him what I just told you, and 'thank you,' he said, and 'what are you doing next Saturday?' he asked, 'you must ride with us!'"

At almost the very moment Yezid said this, Lee's car appeared—a new Mercedes, just traded in and identical in appearance to the last, "except with no scratches or dents," Lee would report. But first he stopped the car near his orchard, and we watched him get out with his camera and take a photograph of a flowering tree that, as Judy affectionately remarked, he'd probably already photographed several dozen times.

I was going to miss the first half of the Tanglewood concert. De nada. Here, in this place that metaphorically in my life had been a mnemonic anchor, I was quite sure I could hear a different kind of music, something composed over many years and in many places, ranging from Mount Kisco to Mount Everest. Its exuberant essence was familiar to anyone who knew the composer, who by my good fortune was just now taking a seat next to me at the table.

Afterword

Lee's Reminiscences and Reflections on Meetings with Ernest Hemingway

I had a total of three direct experiences with E.H. over a period of six years. It was July, 1953, when I first met Hemingway with some friends near Pamplona. We had stayed outside of Pamplona because of the crowds and went to a town called Lecumberri, a village 30 kilometers north of Pamplona where Juanito Quintano had the Hotel Ayesteran, (Juanito was an old friend of Hemingway from the Spanish civil war period). I went over to the hotel on a hot evening around 10:00 pm with my friends. It was a brief meeting, and I am quite sure he did not remember me in any way. I was just a kid, and although I had been indirectly introduced through Sydney Franklin (the bullfighter and an old friend of E.H.), I was just one of a number of people who was interested in shaking hands with this great writer, who had come back to Spain for the first time since the civil war.

The second meeting was in April 1957 when I was armed with a letter of introduction from Carlos Baker of Princeton University who was keenly aware of my interest in Hemingway and in his work. Professor Baker, a major biographer of E.H., arranged the introduction for me as well as some other students at Princeton. At that time I interviewed E.H. at Finca Vigia in Cojimar one morning when the breezes from the Gulf Stream were in perfect harmony with the beautiful sunny day.

E.H. was in good spirits and had just come in from boxing with some friends. He met me in his study on the first floor, and we had a long chat about "men of action" and whether or not (in answer to one of my questions) Hemingway considered himself an existentialist. E.H. was engaging and quite responsive to my questions. He appeared receptive to the eager enquiries of a young man who was then not even 21 years old, but already highly idealistic and involved in adventure and in his own search for meaning. E. H. offered me coffee and invited me to stay for lunch with some of his other friends who either were staying at the Finca or who were coming in from Havana.

The next time I saw Hemingway was during July 1959, when I bumped into the Hemingway entourage while E.H. was covering a series of bullfights for *Life Magazine*. These were later published in book form under the title "The Dangerous Summer" with an admiring foreword by James Michener. I first joined the group of camp followers in Madrid and followed E.H. around for almost 2 weeks from Madrid to Andalusia. In Madrid, "Papa" was staying at the Hotel Suecia. He remembered our encounter in Cuba. He invited me to lunch, and when I arrived in the dining room of the hotel, he and a large group were already at the table. The only person I recognized in Hemingway's entourage was Aaron Hotchner. The others were all strangers. I remember that a pleasant-looking French woman called Monique Lange was present, along with her young daughter, and that Papa recommended a novel she had written recently called Les Plantanes.

After Madrid the entourage picked up and included people like Orson Welles, Irving (Swifty) Lazar, (the famous theatrical agent), Deborah Kerr, Harry Kurnitz, (the screenwriter and playwright) Slim Hawks (later to be married to Leland Hayward and finally to Lord Keith), and Irwin Shaw, the writer. Although people split off and went in different locations from day to day, the basic direction was South, and in mid July, the group encamped in Malaga after a corrida (bullfight) that Sunday afternoon. On July 21, a number of people were invited by Bill Davis, the American expatriate, to festivities at his beautiful villa, La Consula, where he feted Hemingway on his 60th birthday. I was not invited, but learned about the events the following morning at breakfast. Evidently, Antonio Ordonez, the famous bullfighter, who was Hemingway's favorite in Antonio's mano a mano rivalry with his brother-in-law, Luis Miguel Dominguin, held a cigarette in his mouth which Hemingway shot from 100 feet away.

From Malaga the group moved to Algeciras for a major bullfight in which Luis Miguel was featured. Algeciras is anything but a typical Andalusian town. Like Malaga, it is an important seaport, but unlike Malaga, even the old quarter is functional and ugly: flat-roofed buildings crowd narrow streets, and only the broad avenue that borders the waterfront had a certain mercantile grandeur.

In Dominguin's time, the bullring was on the other end of the town, but now, decades later, it has been replaced by a modern structure double in size, and beyond it is a new barrio of high-rise tenements as ungainly as those that have sprung up all over Spain.

During the July feria, the grounds are cluttered with a ferris wheel, dodge 'em cars, and all the other worn mechanical paraphernalia that moves from town to town during the summer season, following the same itinerary as the toreros, who offer a more expensive diversion.

On that Sunday afternoon, Dominguin dedicated his second bull to Mary and Papa. I remember that Papa and Mary went to pay their respects to Dominguin after the corrida, and, as always, his presence caused a stir. I remember that he stayed only a short while, knowing that as soon as Luis Miguel had "cooled out," he would want to bathe and dress and get back on the road. The Hemingways, too, were anxious to be on their way, as they were meeting Ordonez at his ranch near Medina-Sidonia. I met the Hemingways briefly at the bar and told Papa that I had to return to the States to begin law school.

Hemingway expressed astonishment that I would not be present for the major part of the bullfight season (which traditionally is in August), especially as it was now certain that Ordonez and Dominguin would be fighting on the same card within a week. I joked and said that Luis Miguel would be able to "soldier on" without me. "Yeah, I guess he will," Papa replied with a grin, "but we'll miss you, kid." Both he and Mary said that they were anxious to have me at their new home in Ketchum, Idaho, at Thanksgiving time. That was the last time I saw either Papa or Mary.

In early November, 1959 Mary called to tell me that Papa had entered the Mayo Clinic and that the Thanksgiving festivities were cancelled and for me not to come. Ironically, Antonio Ordonez, who was also invited, never got the message not to come, and he arrived only to confront the unhappy situation whereupon he promptly went to Mexico. It was only in July, 1994 when I was in Sun Valley to attend the wedding of my former law professor that I visited the Hemingway house which was left primarily in the state at which it existed at Papa's death. Then I saw the room which I was supposed to occupy on that ill-fated Thanksgiving holiday. In this sense, I finally completed the circle and was glad.

A HEMINGWAY EVENING

Aston Magna - May 6, 1995

PART I

Dialogue I	
Sea Change	Read by George Coyne, Charlotte Hampden and Jean Claude Van Itallie
On Writing	Read by Lynn Nesbit
The Sun Also Rises	Read by George Coyne, Herbert Gould, Jane Iredale Jill Spalding, Ivo Lederer, Jean Claude Van Itallie, Michael Lederer and Lee Elman

INTERMISSION AND DINNER

PART II

The Nick Adams Stories	Read by Jim Hatch, Charlotte Hampden and Chauncey Loomis
Dialogue II	
Hills Like White Elephants	Herbert Gould and Charlotte Hampden
On Nature	Read by Kitty Carlisle Hart
On Love	Read by Jill Spalding/Lee Elman, and Ivo Lederer
Today is Friday	Read by Herbert Gould, Michael Lederer, Bruce Kelly and Lee Elman
On War	Read by Herbert Gould
On Bullfighting	Read by Jim Hatch
On Death and Defiance	Read by Herbert Gould and Jean Claude Van Itallie

Lee's Malraux Connection

I have said for a long time that two people, both twentieth century writers, had a great influence in my intellectual development, first as a younger man but also later in my life. One was Hemingway and the other was Andre Malraux.

I had read intensively most of Malraux's work, in English translation and also quite thoroughly in French, while I was at Princeton. And he was still writing important works even after I graduated. In so many ways, he had a fascinating pull on me, which continues today. I reveled in reading his later works, which had a great impact and influence on my thinking and in my characterization of myself as a living existentialist.

Rightly or wrongly, I would identify with him and follow his intellectual and amorous developments closely. in particular during the period when he wrote his now famous trilogy on the history and influence of art called *Les Voix de Silence* (*The Voices of Silence*), his memoirs (which he called *Anti-Memoires*), his late thinking in *The Chestnut Trees of Altenburg*, and a series of essays about human existence. It was also the time when his personal relationship with the well-known literary priestess in France, Louise de Vilmorin, began to flourish.

I felt I needed to meet him and exchange ideas if he deigned to talk to me. And so, in 1959, I pursued a meeting when I was a Fulbright Scholar in Bologna. I had no connection with someone who knew him or could even give me a letter of introduction, as I had from Carlos Baker who arranged a formal meeting for me with Hemingway. I had to invent or concoct an introduction.

The opportunity came when I learned that Malraux, who had been appointed Minister of Culture by De Gaulle in the Fifth Republic, was to represent the Pavillon Francais at the Bienal of São Paulo in September 1959.

I happened to be in Brazil at that time. I had pursued a relationship with a lovely Brazilian in Italy and Greece. had followed her back to her native land, and she eventually became my first wife.

I knew one of the Commissioners of the Bienal and persuaded him to tell me when Malraux might be free between meetings, so that I could make a cold approach to him.

With this information, I found him one afternoon when he was on a stroll from the French Pavillon to another area of the Bienale campus.

I confronted him on his walk, introduced myself to him and his charming wife, the already famous concert pianist, Madeleine Malraux. She was Andre's brother's widow, and she had a son, Andre's nephew, whom he had adopted.

I immediately engaged him in a kind of interview, in French of course, as Malraux spoke little English. I asked him all sorts of questions about his prolific writings, most of which I was fortunate to have read.

And as I always do with well known writers, I asked him which of his work was the most important to him.

He responded that it was *The Voices of Silence*, which he had just finished. However, I said what I meant was which book overall was the most important for him, and he immediately answered that it was *La Voie Royale* (*The Royal Way*), which he wrote in 1925, about his experiences discovering Angkor Wat in Cambodia. "Il faut y aller," he added—"you must go there," which I did almost 50 years later.

After that semi-chanced and semi-contrived meeting in São Paulo in September 1959, an epistolary relationship developed with this great man which continued until his death in 1976. It was marked by a number of meetings with him at the Ministere de Culture in Paris, where we discussed a wide ranging spectrum of topics from which I derived great satisfaction.

The relationship was a rich one although it was more reserved than that which I enjoyed with Hemingway. It was far more formal, but still very exciting for a young man who was thrilled to be in the awesome presence of one the greatest writers and human beings of the twentieth century.

The story has a pleasing ending. After Malraux died, I thought I had lost contact entirely with his family. However, in early 2005 I met Alain, his nephew and adopted son. We became good friends and he invited me to a wonderful luncheon with his mother in their Paris apartment. Not only did Mme Madeleine Malraux remember me warmly from our encounter in São Paulo in 1959, but, already in her late eighties, she gave me a beautiful one-hour private piano concert in her lovely apartment overlooking the Eiffel Tower [see photo on page 72].

A Friend's Toast at Robert Burns's Birthday

For those of you who've returned again and again to these wonderful Robert Burns dinners and for those of you who are experiencing one for the first time, I'm guessing that you all have the same burning question. Why does Lee do it? We all know that Lee likes to celebrate. Christmas, Chanukah, Passover, Easter, birthdays, real and imagined, weddings, divorces, independence day in Chad. But why has he stuck so loyally to the Robert Burns birthday celebration given the risks of doing anything in January in the Berkshires? I gave this some considerable thought and then did some undercover research. What my research turned up was fascinating and shall now be revealed. The reason is that Robert Burns and Lee Elman have led extremely similar lives and so the *simpatico* Lee must feel for the great bard motivates everything.

Many of you know that Burns was born in 1759 in South Ayrshire, Scotland to a hard-working tenant farmer. Burns was the eldest of seven children. He grew up in poverty and hardship, had little schooling and got most of his education from his father and the parish church. The farm work was so grueling that it eventually broke his health and he died at the age of 37.

"So how could this have anything to do with Lee?" I hear you ask.

You wouldn't be asking it if you hadn't swallowed all the marketing hype. For example, you probably think that Lee was born in Manhattan on Park Avenue and went to some fancy school like Yale. For those of us who've done our research, we know better. Lee was, in fact, born in Mount Kisco, Arkansas to a hard-working chicken farmer. Yes, Lee has spent the rest of his life trying to disguise his accent. In fact, Lee's life on the farm, including shoveling copious amounts of manure, left him with an aversion to chicken that is evident today. Have you ever seen chicken served at an Aston Magna dinner?

How did this erudite, sophisticated art-loving, multi-linguist we see before us get to where he is? Well, like Burns, Elman was mostly home-schooled with the occasional help from outside influences like the local synagogue. And there was a friend named Black who developed his art appreciation and Rosetta Stone took care of the languages. But farm work for Burns and Elman was the principal activity and this is where they both learned to appreciate the opposite sex. Burn's first poem was dedicated to Nelly Kilpatrick in 1774, called "Handsome Nell."

> Once I lov'd a bonie lass.
> Ay, and I love her still;
> And whilst that virtue warms my breast,
> I'll love my handsome Nell.

Eventually, Burns and Lee both left farming for city life and here is where their paths separated. Burns fathered 12 children in his lifetime with a number out of wedlock. As of today, he has over 600 living descendants. Lee, on the other hand, in spite of his early declaration, has led a chaste and almost celibate life. He did spend some time recently improving his thrust but I think that had more to do with his fencing skills.

Still the similarities abound—their love of music, their prowess with languages, Burns learned French and Latin. Lee speaks Italian, French and German, as long as he has the microphone in his ear. And then, of course, their appreciation of good food. I give you, Burn's famous "Ode to a haggis" where he couldn't resist comparing it to a pair of nicely-rounded buttocks. And, of course their reverence and appreciation for things of the past. Burns used to collect songs from what he called "the olden time" often being the first to write down lyrics that had only been passed orally for centuries. This is true of one of the most beloved songs of all time, Auld Lang Syne (Yes, it's Syne by the way and not Zyne.) I want to read you the original, but first, what does auld lang syne mean? Literally translated, it means old, long since but it's commonly translated as "the good old days."

> *Should Old Acquaintance be forgot,*
> *And never thought upon?*
> *The flames of love extinguished,*
> *And fully past and gone?*
> *Is thy sweet heart now grown so cold,*
> *That loving breast of thine;*

That thou canst never once reflect
On auld lang long syne? (The good old days.)
On auld lang syne my Jo,
On auld lang syne,
That thou canst never once reflect,
On auld lang syne?

Clearly, here was a lover who thought Jo was going to be kept happy looking back on a couple of candlelit dinners and a new milking stool. Burns, of course, took it to a new level and asked the question, "Is it right to let old times be forgotten? Shouldn't we remember long-standing friendships?" Is this sounding more and more like Lee and the treasured memories he's given us at Aston Magna? Here is Burn's version where I think it's clear he's turned Jo into a male buddy as he remembers "the good old days" —auld lang syne, a phrase he loved.:

Should old acquaintance be forgot,
And never brought to mind?
Should old acquaintance be forgot,
And auld lang syne?
For aud lang syne, my dear,
For auld lang syne,
We'll take a cup of kindness yet,
For auld lang syne.

Thank you for all the good times, Lee.

—Jane Iredale, January 2014

The Aston Magna Festival

The mission of the Aston Magna Foundation is to enrich the appreciation of music of the past and the understanding of the cultural, political, and social contexts in which it was composed and experienced. The goal is to reach a larger public through the use of historical instruments and practices in performances, recordings, and workshops, and through innovative interdisciplinary educational programs, publications, and electronic media.

Aston Magna's international concert performances have included appearances at the Valtice Festival in the Czech Republic and a European tour of Handel's oratorio, *The Triumph of Time and Truth*, at venues in Europe such as the Pamphilj Palace in Rome, where the work was first heard under Handel's direction in 1707.

Aston Magna seeks to interpret the music of the past as the composer imagined it. Original period instruments—or historically accurate reproductions—are essential performance elements. Performance techniques are appropriate to the period, national styles, culture and aesthetics of the time.

Aston Magna pursues these goals in its educational and public programs, recordings and books. For two decades, the Aston Magna Academies brought together artists and scholars in all disciplines of the humanities for three weeks of intensive interdisciplinary exploration. Two books based on the themes of the Academies have been published. *Schubert's Vienna*, is available through Yale University Press, and *The Worlds of Johann Sebastian Bach* is available through Amadeus Press.

Aston Magna's growing discography includes performances of the Schubert Octet and Mozart Quintets on the Harmonia Mundi label; *The Musical Offering* and other works by J.S. Bach, Bach cantatas as well as Handel's *Triumph of Time and Truth*, Mozart quintets and Monteverdi's landmark opera, *L'Orfeo*, on the Centaur label.

Acknowledgments

My greatest thanks are to all the people in this book, none more so than Lee, whose combination of hospitality, openness, intelligence, engagement, curiosity, and bonhomie is without parallel in my experience.

Wary of forgetting someone—apologies extended in advance—I also wish to thank, for encouragement and readings of portions of the manuscript, Christopher Vyce at the Brattle Agency; Irina Kareva of the Tanglewood Festival Chorus and the Newman-Lakka Institute for Personalized Cancer Care; my brother Nils, a composer and pianist; and my college classmate and fellow writer Stuart Schoffman. Thanks also to my daughters Anna Vigeland and Maren Vigeland, Stanley Rabinowitz, Kim Townsend, Richard Todd, Tracy Mehr, Wayne Kabak, Doug George, Ina Backman, Richard Miller, David Fergusson, Charles Mirotznik, Herbert Gould and Mary Ann Murphy.

To the incomparable Steve Strimer and all my friends at Levellers Press, for your great care and exemplary craft in a literary world too often governed by marketing platforms: grazzissimo!

I began this book while working on another. My visit to Tanglewood on the day I met Lee coincided with some Berkshires geographic research I was doing relative to a novel, *Blue Notes*, that takes place at that bucolic center of music. And so a final thanks to the ghosts of Hawthorne and Mozart, both of whom make appearances in the novel.